Joh.

372.7 Bo

Encou...
: the i... P9-CRW-487
Michael J. Bosse and Jennifer V.
Rotigel.

Feb 2007

32487008828270
NEWARK PUBLIC LIBRARY-NEWARK, OHIO 43055

Encouraging Your Child's
Math Talent

Encouraging Your Child's
Math Talent

The Involved Parents' Guide

Michael J. Bossé, Ph.D.
and Jennifer V. Rotigel, Ed.D.

Prufrock Press Inc.
Waco, Texas

Library of Congress Cataloging-in-Publication Data

Bossé, Michael J., 1960–
   Encouraging your child's math talent: the involved parents' guide / Michael J. Bossé
and Jennifer V. Rotigel.
      p. cm.
   Includes bibliographical references.
   ISBN 1-59363-184-7 (pbk.)
   1. Mathematics—Study and teaching—Parent participation—United States. I. Rotigel, Jennifer V. (Jennifer Vickers), 1953– II. Title.
   QA135.6.B666 2006
   372.7—dc22
                              2005034871

© 2006 Prufrock Press Inc.
All Rights Reserved.

Edited by Lacy Elwood
Layout and cover design by Marjorie Parker

ISBN-13: 978-1-59363-184-0
ISBN-10: 1-59363-184-7

No part of this book may be reproduced, translated, stored in a retrieval system, or trans-
mitted, in any form or by any means, electronic, mechanical, photocopying, microfilm-
ing, recording, or otherwise, without written permission from the publisher.

Printed in the United States of America.

At the time of this book's publication, all facts and figures cited are the most current
available. All telephone numbers, addresses, and Web site URLs are accurate and active.
All publications, organizations, Web sites, and other resources exist as described in the
book, and all have been verified. The authors and Prufrock Press Inc., make no warranty
or guarantee concerning the information and materials given out by organizations or
content found at Web sites, and we are not responsible for any changes that occur after this book's publication. If you find an error, please contact Prufrock Press Inc. We
strongly recommend to parents, teachers, and other adults that you monitor children's
use of the Internet.

PRUFROCK PRESS INC.
P.O. Box 8813
Waco, Texas 76714-8813
(800) 998-2208
http://www.prufrock.com

Contents

— Chapter **1** —
Recognizing Advanced Mathematical Ability in Your Child   15

— Chapter **2** —
Navigating the School System in Support of Your Mathematically Advanced Child   43

— Chapter **3** —

— Chapter **4** —

— List of **Tables & Figures** —

Acknowledgements

The authors wish to acknowledge the vignette contributions of the following people. To maintain the willingness of contributors to openly discuss their situations, names are not associated with various contributions. Thanks to Kira Anderson, Martin Bidegaray, Linda Conlon, Sarah Conway, Mallory Freeberg, Grace Frick, Dave Gambler, Kevan Gray, Marcella Lantzman, Nathan McWherter, Neil Meredith, Brigid Mooney, Darcee Schmidt, Damaris Shaw, Trevor Stabb, Daniel Rotigel, Michael Rotigel, Elaina Marie Swartzlander, Valerie Vrable, Scott Vrable, and Lindsay Beth Willett. Several others have asked that their names not be included, and the authors respect their wishes.

Additionally, we would like to acknowledge the work of Edward Shephard, a graduate assistant at Indiana University of Pennsylvania, for his assistance on the resources section of this book.

Introduction

Parents, this is not a math book. This is a book written for you and your mathematically advanced child. Although we are professional educators, we are also parents and our focus for this book can be stated simply: It is written by parents and for parents. Some of the recommendations provided in this book for parents come from our experiences as parents and others originate through our combined decades of experience in public and private K–12 schools and university settings.

This book looks at various topics that affect parents of mathematically talented students. Some of these include:

- recognizing advanced mathematical ability in your child,
- navigating the school system in support of your mathematically advanced child,
- supporting your mathematically advanced child at home,
- encouraging children to discover mathematics on their own,
- using technology to support mathematically talented students, and
- enrichment opportunities for your mathematically advanced child.

There are many different terms that may be used to describe children who demonstrate ability beyond that shown by other children their age. This ability may be in a particular subject area or it may be demonstrated more generally. *Gifted, talented, academically advanced, promising,* and *demonstrating gifted behaviors* are some of the more commonly used terms. In this book, we will use these terms interchangeably when we refer to a child whose mathematical ability is advanced. We are concerned with offering support and encouragement to children who are interested in mathematics and to parents who wish to know more about helping their children, regardless of the label that is applied by a psychologist or the school system. Similarly, in this book we will use the words *his* and *her* interchangeably, as mathematical ability is shared by both genders.

Mathematically advanced students and their parents and teachers have provided the vignettes, or short articles and stories found throughout the book, to compliment our perspectives. Particularly poignant are the vignettes from students who have had many of the experiences discussed in this book.

Before we talk about how you can support your mathematically interested children, you should think about two important questions:
- Does your child need or deserve additional help?
- Will your child benefit from additional help or challenge?

Being able to answer the first question empowers you to work with the public school system, as well as with other educational providers, while answering the second question may avoid a great deal of strife in the home.

Does Your Child Need or Deserve Additional Help?

Your child is already bright, even advanced, and possibly academically strong. He can do mathematics and even likes mathematics. She may achieve high scores on mathematics tests. He may be in line for scholarships that most other students can only dream about. She may have aspirations for career fields for which few other adults could aim. Some would argue that your child already is blessed and that the limited resources of the school system would be better spent on the students who are not yet meeting the basic academic competencies.

Philosophically, we believe unequivocally that every child has the right to learn new content and skills every day. No child should be bored or forced to march in place while waiting for his classmates to learn material he has already mastered. It is important for you to know that educators and researchers have come to the same conclusion, and you can and should use this information to advocate with the schools on your child's behalf. There are two primary documents that form the rationale supporting the argument that your mathematically advanced child *deserves* additional resources, the Gifted Program Standards and the *Principles and Standards for School Mathematics*. The first resource discusses gifted education and the second book concerns mathematics education. From the two documents it can be argued that advanced mathematics students have an undeniable right to the educa-

Our school has told us that even though our daughter is achieving several years above her grade level they won't accelerate her or help alleviate her boredom. They say we should be happy our daughter is smart so she can learn things easily. The district is only concerned about state testing results so they help the lower achieving students.
—Parent

tional resources needed to further their learning and academic progress.

Gifted Education

The Gifted Program Standards published by the National Association for Gifted Students (NAGC; 1998) is a brief document that details standards that should be met by schools and districts for their programs for gifted students. This document has been developed for children who have been given the label *gifted* by their schools or by outside psychologists, but the basic requirements of a strong and appropriate program are much the same for a child who is advanced in math but not labeled as gifted.

As described by the standards, gifted programs must be developed through significant planning, and not only must the gifted program be internally sound, it must work in tandem with the entire school program. Furthermore, it should not be simply an extracurricular add-on; it should be thoroughly integrated with the existing school environment. Students and parents should not find that the students must leave the school premises or wait until after school for programs, curricula, and instruction that meet the needs of the advanced student. Additional resources, whether they are curricular, technological, material, or instructional in nature, also should be provided to the gifted programs. Programs lacking sufficient resources will not adequately meet the needs of academically advanced students.

This year, I've been teaching a small group of children who are talented in math, and it is really great to see how they challenge each other. I know that they look forward to our class, and I can make good progress with them since they are on approximately the same level and I can adjust the pace. —Teacher

In addition, the Gifted Program Standards state that within one or more subjects, the curriculum, instructional techniques, projects assigned, learning opportunities, pacing of materials, and many other factors should be individualized for students as needed. While this sounds overly complex to maintain within a school, one must remember that the number of gifted students within such programs in most schools is relatively small. Altogether, the Gifted Program Standards make a compelling argument: Your child deserves to get more if he or she needs more in order to reach his fullest potential. When parents must argue for school systems to provide their child with appropriate resources not only to survive but also to thrive, they need the backing of educational documents that are respected by all. From the perspective of gifted education, you can utilize the Gifted Program Standards to support your case.

Mathematics Education

Mathematics education also has a set of national standards. The book, *Principles and Standards for School Mathematics,* published by the National Council of Teachers of Mathematics (NCTM; 2000) provides standards for K–12 mathematics education in the U.S. So significant is the *Principles and Standards* to the national stage that most states have adopted these recommendations (with only slight modifications) as their own curricula, goals, and standards.

NCTM's Web site (http://www.nctm.org) publishes a number of philosophical statements within its Position Statements section. These statements are intended to inform the public, educators, and policymakers about NCTM's core beliefs and its positions on certain issues. One of these statements reads, "Every student should have equitable and optimal opportunities to learn mathematics free from bias—intentional or unintentional—based on race, gender, socioeconomic status, or language" (NCTM, 2005, ¶ 1).

Furthermore, in the introduction of its *Principles and Standards*, NCTM promotes the following vision:

> Imagine a classroom, a school, or a school district where all students have access to high-quality, engaging mathematics instruction. There are ambitious expectations for all, with accommodation for those who need it. Knowledgeable teachers have adequate resources to support their work and are continually growing as professionals. The curriculum is mathematically rich, offering students opportunities to learn important mathematical concepts and procedures with understanding. Technology is an essential component of the environment.
>
> Students confidently engage in complex mathematical tasks chosen carefully by teachers. They draw on knowledge from a wide variety of mathematical topics, sometimes approaching the same problem from different mathematical perspectives or representing the mathematics in different ways until they find methods that enable them to make progress. Teachers help students make, refine, and explore conjectures on the basis of evidence and use a variety of reasoning and proof techniques to confirm or disprove those conjectures.
>
> Students are flexible and resourceful problem solvers. Alone or in groups and with access to technology, they work productively and reflectively, with the skilled guidance of their teachers. Orally and in writing, students communicate their ideas and results effectively. They value mathematics and engage actively in learning it. (NCTM, 2000, p. 3)

Parents can be assured that no national, state, or county educational philosophies will suggest that advanced students receive fewer resources than average students. No standards will advocate that the curriculum for the average child is appropriate, in similar form, for advanced students. In fact, almost all the national and state standards recommend that advanced students receive some modification of the curriculum to best meet their needs. To summarize the current prevailing philosophy of education, one could say that equity does not mean that all students get the same education; but rather that every student gets the education they need.

Summarily, the Gifted Program Standards and the *Principles and Standards* speak with one voice declaring that *all* students deserve what they need to fulfill their academic potential, and this is no less so for mathematically advanced students.

We have now cleared one hurdle. We can now agree that all students *deserve* the resources and educational opportunities to meet their academic potential. However, do all academically advanced students *need* additional resources and educational opportunities? In order to answer this, we must carefully distinguish between students *surviving* the educational system and career pursuits and students *thriving* in these endeavors. Our goals for these advanced students determine our goals for their education. If it is acceptable for talented students to become little more than average, then they need nothing in addition to what is given to average students. However, if we value all humanity and hope to see each individual meet his or her fullest potential in school and in life, then we can argue that mathematically talented students indeed need the resources and programs that would allow them to develop to their full potential.

Will Your Child Benefit From Additional Help and Academic Challenge?

Surprisingly, mathematical ability does not automatically translate into mathematical interest. Mathematically advanced children may or may not be more interested in the study of mathematics than other subject areas. Simply because a subject comes easy to a student does not mean he likes it more than others.

As many parents know, students who do not do well in school may still have high academic ability. Some students perform well in scholastic endeavors with minimal effort and lackluster interest, and extremely intelligent students may often be disinterested with traditional schooling. This academic disinterest may cause friction and affect the home life of the entire family. If your child has strong mathematical ability but seems to be disinterested in math, you may become frustrated by your attempts to influence your child's interest in math. It is important to remember that children grow and develop at different rates and change dramatically from one year to the next. You should be careful not to be too pushy as this can cause a child to turn off completely.

> I know that my daughter is talented in math, but she seems to be very happy just learning whatever her friends do in the regular classroom. I think she is good at so many things that she is willing to just let math be an easy subject for her so she has more time for other subjects right now.
> —Parent

A variety of circumstances may lead mathematically advanced students to underachieve or lack interest in math. First, these students may not be sufficiently challenged by the mathematics content available to them. Research demonstrates that K–12 students struggle most with reading, writing, and mathematics, and many struggle uniquely with mathematics. However, because mathematically advanced students do not struggle with the subject, they are often found to be academically competent in all other scholastic subjects, as well. Second, mathematically talented students may not see the math topics studied in school as relevant to their lives. Lastly, they may have other interests in their lives they see as far more meaningful and significant than the pursuit of mathematics.

It is important for you to judiciously select when and how to motivate your children in order to increase their mathematical interest and endeavors. If your mathematically advanced child is disinterested in pursuing math further than the school's curriculum, you should try to figure out why. This understanding of your child's perspective is necessary if you are going to select effective enhancement opportunities for him.

Occasionally, mathematically advanced children have skills and understanding that far surpass those of their parents, and they resent their parent's involvement and interpret it as invasive. On other occasions, these advanced students are already self-directed learners. They have come to recognize educators as mere obstacles to their own pursuits and interests. Again, you must know your child well and know how to positively stimulate him to further study. It is equally important for you to know when to back off and let your child decide what interests to pursue.

You yourself may be mathematically advanced, have a career in mathematics or the sciences, and feel you are

> I have always loved mathematics and have endured a great deal of personal vilification for it. But, I have also had great jobs. My educational experiences were excellent and exciting. I wish my son shared my interest. He has far more ability than I did, but wants to do other things instead. I support him in his other interests, but I am concerned that he will not have the career options that I have had. —Parent

able to competently assist your children at home. However, parental mathematical ability does not automatically create an environment in the home conducive to parents mentoring their children in mathematics. In fact, many parents report that seemingly anyone other than themselves can more effectively tutor their children. Friction between parents and children regarding academic performance seems to occur more often than not. Additionally, just because adults are mathematically advanced does not necessarily indicate that they are in touch with the K–12 curricula used in schools today.

Parental Involvement and Expectations

Clearly, you want the very best for your child and hope that she will excel in mathematics. Most parents, having experienced high school, some college, and employment, realize that some scholastic subjects are gateways to and from various career fields. For example, if a person can't write well, they will be unable to select from the many career opportunities that demand extensive writing and communication skills. Mathematics has also been recognized as a gatekeeper subject, as the National Council of Teachers of Mathematics notes:

> In this changing world, those who understand and can do mathematics will have significantly enhanced opportunities and options for shaping their futures. Mathematical competence opens doors to productive futures. A lack of mathematical competence keeps those doors closed. (NCTM, 2000, p. 5)

No parent wants his or her child to be limited in future career choices, and you certainly want to make mathematics your child's ally, rather than enemy, in the pursuit for employment. Regardless of your own mathematical ability and feelings toward math, you should understand its value in opening various pathways for your child.

This book seeks to offer realistic solutions to parents in respect to their own mathematical abilities, interests, and confidence. The level, degree, and direction of your involvement and expectations for your support of your child are somewhat contingent upon your mathematical ability, confidence, and background. Therefore, one size does not fit all. Understanding that some parents can help in some ways while others can help in different ways goes far to alleviate the fear, frustration, and guilt parents sometimes feel when helping their children with math.

> My parents remained supportive of me and my efforts in math. The greatest encouragement I received from them was praise for every one of my accomplishments. They also forgave me when I made mistakes, such as a low grade on an assignment, and they never once forced me into an advanced course. My parents let me decide each time whether or not to take the higher level class. —University Student

As the mathematical skills and background of parents differ, so should the type of support you seek to provide to your mathematically advanced child. Some parents will be able to independently provide rich, provocative mathematical supplementation to their children; some will not. If you don't feel confident in providing direct mathematical assistance to your child yourself, many resources are available to help you. If you do possess the mathematical ability to independently assist your child, these resources may help to extend your perspective.

In the next few chapters, we will investigate how to recognize if your child is mathematically advanced, what you can do to support your child in school, what you can do to support her at home, and resources that are available to parents and students.

> I still count on my fingers, and I have no idea what my son is talking about with his math. I really feel inadequate and wish he were interested in something that I am good at! When the teacher tries to explain what they are doing in school, I just nod and pretend that I understand.
> —Parent

Summary of Key Points

- Children will not reach their potential if the educational experiences they receive are not matched with their educational needs, ability, and interests.
- The NAGC Gifted Program Standards detail recommendations for schools regarding programs for gifted children.
- The NCTM *Principles and Standards* describes recommendations for mathematics education and includes information for educators of talented students.
- Parents should determine whether their child wants more challenge in mathematics than he is currently experiencing.

Questions for Parents to Ask Their Child

- What do you want to be when you grow up?
- How much do you like math?
- Would you like to have a career in mathematics?
- Is the math you are studying in school interesting and challenging?
- Would you like to study math relating to some of your hobbies?

- Do you wish to spend more time learning more mathematics?
  - How much time per week?
  - Would you like to study on your own or with someone else?
- If we got you some extra help from someone, would you remain committed to it?
- Would you be willing to go to someone's office or to a university to learn more?

Questions for Parents to Ask Themselves

- Do I want to provide my child with more mathematical experiences?
- Do I agree with educational documents stating that mathematically advanced children both need and deserve additional educational resources and experiences?
- Am I willing to support (financial, transportation, time, etc.) my child in his or her efforts to get more mathematical support?
- Do I think that my child's school is doing all that it can and should to educate my child?
- What can I do to help my child?
- Over the past few years, has my child gained or lost interest in mathematics?
- Is providing more resources and opportunities for my child in math as important to me as providing him or her with opportunities in sports, art, or music?

— *Chapter* **1** —

Recognizing Advanced Mathematical Ability in Your Child

W hen your child seems to be advanced in a particular subject area, it is sometimes hard to know if he is demonstrating average progress and ability, or if he is advanced. Many parents are confused about the difference, because schools frequently introduce mathematical topics in earlier grades than parents expect. Additionally, it is sometimes difficult for parents to know just how much their child is ahead of his classmates.

The following sections will help you to understand how students become recognized by their school as being advanced or gifted in mathematics. Although the focus of this book is mathematically advanced students, it is sometimes very difficult to distinguish between a child who is mathematically advanced and a child who is gifted or talented. The level of mathematical talent or ability that your child has becomes important when you are trying to determine the amount of acceleration or enrichment that she might need. Correctly determining your child's level of ability and potential in mathematics is important and deserves attention. Failing to provide educational experiences that match your child's ability can effectively stunt her academic growth. Forcing your child into classes and experiences that are too advanced for him can provide a negative reaction in your child and cause him to rebel.

The label *gifted* is a legal term that in many states allows a child to receive special services in the school system in order to meet his or her educational needs. The services that are reserved for children who are identified as gifted vary throughout the country, and you may find that your child will need to qualify in order to receive those services. However, in many schools, children who have advanced abilities but are not labeled as gifted can receive the benefits of the programs developed for gifted children.

> I really don't care what people call me. The school calls me talented and students call me a nerd. I like taking advanced courses and I'm glad that I can study more difficult courses than my friends. I can't wait to go to college. I am told that smarter students go into different majors than other students. —Student

A number of recognized tools are accepted throughout the educational community for use in assessing a student's mathematical ability. Unfortunately, you will usually need to go through the educational system or hire a professional psychologist who is experienced in administering and interpreting achievement and ability tests. A comprehensive educational assessment of your child's ability and achievement level will include a variety of tests, observations, and input from a variety of sources. Some of the input will be derived from precise educational testing, while the rest will come from observing your child and his educational progress.

This chapter will consider the following topics:

- Impact of mathematical advancement on the family
- Common vocabulary regarding the mathematically talented, advanced, or gifted
- Characteristics of a mathematically advanced child
- Assessment of achievement and ability
  - o Achievement and above-level testing
  - o Talent searches
  - o Additional assessments
- Issues affecting mathematically talented children
  - o A child's interest in mathematics
  - o Playing with mathematical ideas
  - o Unusual problem-solving strategies
  - o Girls and math

Impact of Mathematical Advancement on the Family

Parents are not always happy to discover that their child is advanced in a subject area. But, who would not want their child to be able to attain skills easily and demonstrate mastery of valuable material at an early age? In some cases, parents recognize that it may be difficult to provide an appropriate program of study for a child who is mathematically talented. Suddenly, there develops a perceived burden of extra responsibility because you might feel that you must find ways to nurture this wonderful gift.

Instead of thinking ahead toward saving money for college, you may fear that a private elementary or secondary school will now be a necessary expense. You may believe that your school system will not provide an appropriate education for your child, and that perhaps you will need to homeschool your child. You may worry that your child will grow up to be weird and not fit in socially. Or, you may be concerned that your own math ability is weak, and therefore you will not be able to keep up with your child. You may feel threatened by the ability demonstrated by your child, and wish to deflect his interest into less academic ventures. These concerns are understandable, because many parents don't know other children or adults who are gifted and may have heard some of the unfounded myths that circulate about gifted individuals. Fortunately, you will find that most of these concerns are unfounded. Table 1 presents some common misconceptions about math and may help relieve your concerns.

Perhaps not surprisingly, children who are academically talented may have some misgivings of their own. In an effort to fit in, your child may camouflage his ability and even neglect his schoolwork so that his grades will not stand out. Girls often feel the need to "act dumb," particularly in the areas of math and science. Middle school brings challenges in the social arena when peer pressure may dictate that children attempt to shine athletically rather than academically. You and your child's school need to work together closely to support and encourage academic excellence and strong educational experiences.

> So far, it has been interesting having a child who is so advanced in mathematics. We are lucky that our school is very helpful and has allowed Jason to accelerate and participate in math enrichment opportunities. I think that we will probably want to look into some summer school or after school math activities for him, though, and I worry about paying for it all. —Parent

In fact, it may be difficult for you to provide the best educational experience for your child. The primary reason for this is that you, with the help of the school and other experts, must first

Table 1
Common Misconceptions
About Learning Mathematics

- **I'm a random, creative right-brain thinker. Math is for analytical, left-brain people.** This argument is common, but entirely incorrect. Many great mathematicians are very creative, and thus, right-brain thinkers. Many mathematicians are also musicians, poets, artists, and writers, and much mathematical learning requires creativity and problem solving. Furthermore, there are many fields of mathematics, and different types of thinkers can find a field of mathematics in which they can excel.

- **I am not interested in mathematics. It is boring and I rarely use it in my real life.** Few people are interested in fields in which they have little exposure, particularly when the exposure they have is disconnected from the concerns of their real lives. When mathematics is demonstrated as a tool by which real-world problems and personal interests can be solved and investigated, people tend to value it more highly and find it to be interesting. The secret to gaining interest in mathematics lies in using mathematics in personal ways and not simply as an academic discipline.

- **I'm a girl, so I can't do math.** Research has repeatedly demonstrated that females learn mathematics at least as well as males. Unfortunately, society may tend to paint a more negative picture, because girls are often directed away from the areas of math and science. When this happens, girls don't get as much exposure to math and have fewer opportunities to develop their mathematical abilities.

- **Mathematics is hard. It is complicated and there are too many rules.** Mathematics is like any other subject where practice and frequent exposure allows the student to become comfortable with the content. Unfortunately, students are rarely shown how the interconnections of the rules make mathematics easier rather than more difficult.

- **I'm too old to learn mathematics, so I can't help my child with it.** Barring some illness, no one is too old to learn mathematics. As is the case with learning anything else, it simply takes time and desire.

- **Mathematics scares me to death.** People often don't like mathematics because of their fears of mathematics. In fact, more adults and children are negatively affected by the fears they harbor about mathematics than by any lack in mathematical ability. Mathphobia has been thoroughly investigated and found to be a real hindrance to learning mathematics.

determine what the optimum educational experience might look like based upon your child's ability. Then you will need to work together with schools, and perhaps outside experts, to create that experience. There may be times when the school, for whatever reason, will not provide adequately for your child and you will feel the need to supplement your child's education with enrichment experiences, tutoring, mentors, summer camps, and so on.

> When I was going through school as a gifted child, I never understood the other kids who were obviously bright, but for some reason always tried to hide it. I understand it much more now after working with children—the peer pressure can be astounding! Teachers can't control every little swerve that social groups take in school, but at least they should make gifted youth feel that it is OK to be yourself. —University Student

Common Vocabulary Regarding Mathematically Advanced and Gifted Students

In order to understand some of the terms educators use in describing children, think about your own classmates from your school years. Some students were below average, the largest group fell into the average range, and some were above average. Within the group of students who were above average in their ability were some students who would be called *advanced* and a few others who had even higher abilities and were termed *gifted*. In this book, we want to help parents of children who are above average in mathematical ability, so we refer to those children as being mathematically advanced. Because a child may be mathematically advanced and also gifted, we have included a bit of information to help you decide if your child may also be gifted.

Although the term *gifted* is used in legislation and in a great deal of educational literature, it is viewed unfavorably by some. Many people are comfortable describing a gifted athlete, but are not happy with saying that someone is gifted in mathematics. School programs for gifted children are often known by an acronym, and children sometimes try not to let everyone know that they belong to the program because they don't want to brag about their ability. While fear of ridicule is not a problem for children who participate in a special choir or sports team, it may be an issue for a child who participates in a gifted academic program.

You may have heard the notion that all children are gifted. While this is a lovely sentiment, it must be acknowledged that not all children learn at the same pace, nor are all children prepared to study subjects in depth before the subject matter is normally introduced in a school's curriculum. Parents and educators must take a pragmatic view and recognize a child's ability, and make provisions in her education to ensure her educational needs are being met. Every child deserves to learn every day. It is not fair or equitable to ask a child to wait patiently for his classmates to catch up while he marks time in boredom or is asked to tutor his peers.

Whether your child is mathematically advanced or mathematically advanced and also gifted should be determined by a comprehensive educational assessment, which we will discuss later in this chapter. However, you should be aware that whatever the level of talent your child has, avoiding the use of descriptive terms or minimizing the child's talent is *not* the way to support your child's mathematical ability. It is important for you to recognize your child's strengths and help nurture them. You may sometimes need to act as your child's advocate and you should not feel the need to apologize or make excuses for the modifications to the educational program that may be necessary for your child to be able to make progress each school day.

Interestingly, your child may be academically advanced in many subjects or just in mathematics. A child who is mathematically advanced may or may not be a superb reader. It is even possible for a child to be advanced in mathematics and not be very interested in learning mathematical content. A child who has high ability in several areas may find that her interest alternates between the areas. This may be due to the influence of an excellent teacher, the particular content being presented, or it may simply be a function of maturation.

It may be very easy for you to recognize that your child is mathematically advanced because you may have seen, through his interactions with his agemates, that he is so obviously beyond his agemates in mathematical interest and achievement. Or, you may be able to use other factors to pinpoint your child's math talent. For example, the first-grade child who is interested in converting decimals to fractions is clearly working beyond his age and grade expectations. You may find that your child remembers numbers easily and loves to play games related to numbers. It can be very exciting to watch a child who is talented in mathematics learn things so easily that it seems to be effortless. Table 2 provides a list of some of the characteristics of mathematically advanced children.

Sometimes, however, your child may report that math is boring and that he is not interested in doing his math schoolwork. This is not necessarily an indication that math is not an area of strength, rather it may be a signal that the math program at school is moving too slowly or your child has already mastered the material being presented. In fact, some children who are talented in math don't achieve good grades in the subject because they solve problems in unusual ways and sometimes cannot (or don't wish to) explain their method of problem solving to the teacher.

Usually, the mathematically advanced child falls somewhere in between these extremes. You may be surprised at the interest your child shows in math games, riddles, and activities. She

Table 2
Characteristics of a Mathematically Advanced Child

Young children often display an ability to do and understand mathematics, and you may be the first to suspect that your child is mathematically advanced. You may notice that your young child:

- can *count* objects;
- demonstrates mathematical thinking such as comparing, sorting, classifying, and finding patterns;
- has an interest in geometric shapes;
- likes to construct things;
- can add and subtract;
- can multiply;
- is continually inquisitive about mathematics;
- is inquisitive about science and how things work;
- enjoys role play in which one or more roles include personalities that use mathematics in their careers;
- openly states that he likes doing math; and
- is not afraid of mathematics.

Once your child enters school, you will have additional information that will give you clues to your child's math ability. Mathematically advanced students demonstrate many common characteristics, and your child may be mathematically advanced if he:

- learns math faster and more efficiently than his classmates;
- learns new math content with few repetitions;
- plays math or video games;
- comes up with unusual ways to solve math problems;
- enjoys solving math problems;
- remembers new math content and uses it easily;
- wants to pursue a topic beyond the grade-level textbook;
- is frustrated by low-level, repetitious homework in math;
- asks theoretical questions that may challenge adults' knowledge of math;
- wants to know *why* the answer is correct; and
- needs significant modification of the school's curriculum in order to make progress.

may be able to make interesting comparisons between numbers or have a strong interest in geometry or measurement. She may get good grades in math and enjoy doing extra challenge problems provided by the teacher. Perhaps she just seems to be able to know the answer without having to work out the problem.

Many parents believe that if their child can do math problems quickly that means that he is mathematically advanced. This is not necessarily the case, because many children can very rapidly perform mathematical computations. However, there is far more to mathematical understanding than getting the answer first. A child with advanced math ability will be able to apply mathematics in appropriate and novel situations, recognize integrated concepts among mathematical topics, be able to explain mathematical principles, and so on.

> Being considered gifted was often both a blessing and a curse. On one hand you were given special treatment and allowed to participate in interesting and exciting events—which meant skipping other classes. But, on the other hand, you were still seg-regated, still considered "different." Gifted and special education kids have a lot in common in this way.
> —Gifted Student

Assessment of Achievement and Ability

You may wonder why it is important to identify and label a child as mathematically advanced or gifted in mathematics. The simplest reason is that the identification and label provide a foundation through which to communicate with teachers, school administrators, and others regarding appropriate educational programs and opportunities. In addition, special programs in schools are often closed to children who are not identified as gifted.

If you or your child's teacher thinks that your child may be academically advanced, a comprehensive educational assessment, including both formal and informal assessments, should be developed and utilized to assist with the identification of your child's ability and to make appropriate educational plans. A great deal of information must be gathered, as the report should include information from parents, teachers, a school psychologist, and school records, as well as any evaluations that have been done outside of the school. The assessment should include:

- present levels of achievement,
- results of psychological testing (IQ and other tests),
- the rate of acquisition of new material (how fast does he learn new concepts?),
- the rate of retention of the content that has already been mastered (how well can he remember new things he has just learned?),
- an indication of particular strengths and weaknesses,
- recommendations for acceleration and enrichment, and
- modifications that are recommended for the regular education program.

While thorough assessment and subsequent academic planning sounds like a complicated endeavor, a careful assessment is essential for several reasons. From the school's perspective, it is important that children whose ability necessitates modification of the regular curriculum be identified and served. Because of the additional costs that may be involved, many schools are careful not to identify as mathematically

After I was diagnosed as gifted, everything changed. I had tougher classes with other smart kids. We got to do all kinds of cool stuff. Sometimes school got too hard, though, and I didn't think it was fair. We worked harder than all the other kids in school. But, I think that it was all worth it.
—Student

gifted those children who are highly achieving but whose needs can be met in the regular program of study. On the other hand, you must be careful to ensure that your child's ability is accurately assessed so that his academic needs will be met.

In many schools, only those children who are labeled as advanced in mathematics will have access to acceleration and enrichment options and individually designed study programs. However, there also may be a few disadvantages that may accompany the label. In some schools, there may be a social stigma connected with being labeled as gifted or talented in mathematics. In addition, some teachers may feel intimidated and actually be unable to provide adequately for these children in their classes. Teachers may hold unreasonable expectations for children who are academically advanced and may even attempt to turn them into teacher's assistants by requiring them to tutor their peers.

> My son's teacher criticized him because he was quiet in class. He told me, "I do answer when the teacher really needs me to help her out. I don't want to put my hand up all of the time so everyone knows that I know all of the answers. I answer her when no one else will."
> —Parent

If your child is already in school, you will probably find that her school will begin its identification efforts with a look at her achievement. Grades in mathematics and science are one measure of achievement, yet it is certainly possible for a mathematically talented child to have average grades in math and/or science. As previously noted, there may be several reasons for this, ranging from low-level content, slow pace of instruction, social factors causing your child to want to hide his ability, your child's neglect of homework assignments, poor teaching techniques, or simply lack of interest in the subject.

Teachers' recommendations and anecdotal records provide further information regarding a child's ability. One problem with this is that elementary school teachers generally receive little or no training in the identification of advanced children or the specialized techniques they should use when teaching them. Certainly the opinions of more highly trained faculty and administrators in respect to mathematically talented students should be sought and should carry more weight. However, research demonstrates that in general, teachers do not accurately identify the advanced children in their classes. Some studies have shown that teachers tend to identify as gifted those children who have learning styles similar to their own. In addition, teachers often believe that the children who answer questions in class are the brightest students.

It is not always easy to convince a school to test a child to determine his educational needs. While some schools do an excellent job at this assessment and subsequent curricular modification, other schools will balk at both the expense of testing and the expense of necessary resources for mathematically advanced children. Nevertheless, parents can argue that their child deserves testing, particularly if an adequate amount of evidence makes a case for mathematical giftedness, and schools should provide reasonable testing.

Achievement Tests and Above-Level Testing

Standardized achievement tests, such as the Iowa Test of Basic Skills, the California Achievement Test, and the Stanford Achievement Test are usually administered to groups of children on a yearly basis by schools in order to measure students' progress. Standardized tests are organized by subject area and divided by grade level. A third-grade child, for example, would typically be given a test near the end of the academic year that includes content that a third grader would be expected to know. One difficulty with this is that sometimes the content of the achievement test does not match the school's curriculum very well, and therefore contains material that the children have not encountered. Alternatively, the test may not include much of what the children actually were taught in the classroom. If there is a significant mismatch between the curriculum of the school and the content being assessed by the achievement test, the results are likely to be less than accurate.

In addition to group achievement tests, individual achievement tests may be administered to students. Examples of individual achievement tests are the Weschler Individual Achievement Test, Kaufman Test of Educational Achievement, and the Woodcock-Johnson achievement tests. Individual achievement tests are usually more accurate than group tests, as the examiner is able to directly observe the child's behavior and control the testing situation.

The results of standardized achievement tests may be used as one indication of a child's achievement in mathematics. Unfortunately, teachers are seldom trained to interpret and use the results of standardized tests, so the test results are often sent home to parents, filed at school, and forgotten. The score reports may be confusing to parents, who may misunderstand the significance of the results. For example, many standardized tests report a grade level equivalent. A third-grade child who performs well in math may earn a grade equivalent of fifth grade. This does not mean that she should be placed in that grade level, but rather that she has scored the way an average fifth grader would on that particular test.

> My son was 9 years old when the school psychologist tested him on 15 different days. I thought it was awful, and he missed so much of his class time. But, when I asked him about it, he told me that he was having a great time! The tests were a lot more fun that the regular class. —Parent

Standardized achievement tests have additional limitations. For example, a child who is in fifth grade is usually given a test for fifth graders, yet talented children often answer all or most of the questions correctly on testing instruments that are designed for children in their particular grade level. When this happens, it is clear that he has high achievement in that subject or subjects, but because he has hit the top of the test (known as the ceiling) by answering all or most of the questions correctly, educators are unable to determine how much more he can do unless he takes an additional test that contains more advanced and difficult items.

High achievement in a particular subject area on a grade-level achievement test is not necessarily an indication of high ability in that area, but simply means that the child has mastered (at a high level) the specific content expected of a child at her grade level. If your child has scored at the 95th percentile or above on one or more subtests of a grade-level standardized test, it is necessary to administer another test of greater difficulty in order to determine if she is able to correctly answer more difficult questions than were included on the grade-level test. This is known as above-level testing. For example, if two children each score in the 95th percentile in the mathematics subtest of a standardized test, that would indicate that both children have high achievement in mathematics compared to other children in their grade level. It would not be possible from this result to determine if both children have similar ability in mathematics, however. Perhaps one of the children would have been able to answer many more complex and advanced questions

> When I got tested in first grade, I went home and complained to my mother who then kept me out of the program because she thought I wouldn't want to miss my regular class. If they had only said what the tests were for I would have expressed my desire to be in the program. —Student

that were not included on the grade-level test. In this situation, above-level testing will be needed.

Above-level testing is simply the administration of an achievement test that was designed for older children. Through the use of above-level testing, it is possible to determine more clearly the extent of mathematical ability as it is being expressed at the time of testing. This is important, because the recommended educational program for a child who is moderately gifted in mathematics should be very different from the recommended program for a child who is extremely gifted in math. The school may administer an above-level achievement test, but it is often necessary for parents to look outside the school for this type of testing. Talent searches generally offer above-level testing for a reasonable fee.

Talent Searches

Dr. Julian Stanley began the first talent search at Johns Hopkins University in 1971 when he founded the Study of Mathematically Precocious Youth (SMPY). Today, there are regional talent searches located throughout the United States, providing many services for academically advanced students (see Table 3.) Located at various colleges and universities, talent searches offer much more than just above-level testing. Services include the interpretation of testing results, national recognition, scholarships to college classes, enrichment programs and summer classes,

In seventh grade my daughter took the SAT through the Johns Hopkins Center for Talented Youth (CTY). Students who scored better than the average for high school seniors were invited to attend CTY's summer academic programs. CTY's challenging coursework gave my daughter an understanding of what she was capable of achieving, but more important was the fact that she found a social community where she belonged. —Parent

Table 3
Talent Searches in the U.S.

Academic Talent Search: California State University, Sacramento, CA

ADVANCE Program for Young Scholars: Natchitoches, LA

Belin-Blank International Center for Gifted Education and Talent Development: University of Iowa, Iowa City, IA

Canada/USA Mathcamp: Cambridge, MA

Carnegie Mellon Institute for Talented Elementary Students: Carnegie Mellon University, Pittsburgh, PA

Center for Talent Development: Northwestern University, Evanston, IL

Center for Talented Youth: Johns Hopkins University, Baltimore, MD

Frances A. Karnes Center for Gifted Studies: University of Southern Mississippi, Hattiesburg, MS

Hampshire College Summer Studies in Mathematics: Hampshire College, Amherst, MA

Math for Young Achievers: University of Wisconsin at Eau Claire, Eau Claire, WI

Office of Precollegiate Programs for Talented and Gifted: Iowa State University, Ames, IA

Pennsylvania Governor's Schools of Excellence: Harrisburg, PA, and throughout Pennsylvania

Program in Mathematics for Young Scientists: Boston University, Boston, MA

Purdue University Gifted Education Resource Institute: Purdue University, West Lafayette, IN

Research Science Institute: Vienna, VA

Rocky Mountain Talent Search and Summer Institute: University of Denver, Denver, CO

Ross Mathematics Program: Ohio State University, Columbus, OH

Southern Methodist University Gifted Students Institute and Precollege Programs: Southern Methodist University, Dallas, TX

Summer Program for Verbally and Mathematically Precocious Youth: Western Kentucky University, Bowling Green, KY

Talent Identification Program: Duke University, Durham, NC

Wisconsin Center for Academically Talented Youth: Madison, WI

University of Minnesota Talented Youth Mathematics Program: University of Minnesota, Minneapolis, MN counseling, and general information regarding acceleration and enrichment options. Appendix G of this book contains a listing of the university-based talent searches and contact information for each.

Most parents initially contact a talent search so that their child may participate in above-level testing. For elementary school aged children, many talent searches offer the EXPLORE test. The EXPLORE was developed for eighth graders, and thus provides enough high difficulty questions so that it is possible to more closely determine an elementary student's ability in a subject area. Curricular areas tested on the EXPLORE include English, mathematics, reading, and science reasoning skills.

You should carefully consider whether your child is mature enough to take an above-level test. Some bright children are quite used to knowing all the answers on tests, and can become very upset when they are presented with a test of significantly higher difficulty. Instead of feeling happy about all of the questions he was able to answer, your child may concentrate on his inability to answer all of the questions. Some children may feel pressured to do well and instead do poorly because of testing anxiety. Research indicates that while third graders should participate in above-level testing only if they are clearly very advanced, fourth-, fifth-, and sixth-grade children usually benefit from the experience. Before your child takes an above-level test, you should carefully explain to him the reasons for the testing and include the expectation that there may be many questions on the test that will be hard for him to answer.

Many talented seventh graders take the SAT through regional talent searches. The SAT was designed for high school juniors and seniors and is used by many colleges and universities in their admissions process, because it has a high correlation with grades earned while in college. Students who score well on the SAT in seventh grade are offered participation in many acceleration and enrichment opportunities, including free college courses, scholarships, and summer schools for academically talented children.

Additional Assessments

Schools usually provide a school psychologist who can administer psychological testing to help determine your child's general ability level. Commonly called an IQ test, this test is designed to measure a child's ability in verbal and performance levels. Most schools require that a child earn a predetermined minimum score on an IQ test in order to be considered for inclusion in a gifted program or to receive modification of the regular curriculum. However, most states require the use of multiple criteria so that a child cannot be denied entrance into a gifted program simply because he has not attained the minimum score a school determines as constituting giftedness on an IQ test.

In addition to administering an IQ test, the school psychologist should attempt to determine your child's rate of acquisition of new material and the rate of retention of material that has been mastered. In some cases this information is gained through testing by the school psychologist, and in other situations, the psychologist interviews your child's teachers. A classroom observation is often included as part of the comprehensive assessment, and the psychologist usually will report on things such as your child's demeanor during class time, participation (or lack of it), and your child's general level of engagement with his learning environment.

Your observations as a parent are a very important part of the information that needs to be gathered, so you should be interviewed and your information should be included in the report.

You know your child better than anyone and have spent a considerable amount of time in one-on-one situations with him in a wide variety of settings. You should try to list specific things you have noticed about your child's mathematics ability. It is also helpful to save papers and projects that he has completed.

Issues Affecting Mathematically Advanced Children

In education, we are interested in learning, thinking, and using ideas; educators and psychologists call this the *cognitive realm*. In addition, there are other factors that affect learning, such as feelings, interest, motivation, fear, competition, and many other factors that are more emotional than cognitive. These other factors belong to the *affective realm*, and it is clear that children learn best when they are both interested in the subject matter and emotionally comfortable with the work. In fact, a student's academic performance can be stunted by her own emotional makeup or by psychological, sociological, and emotional environmental factors.

Many affective issues impact learning. Because of this, we can also use some observable affective issues as a part of an informal assessment regarding mathematical talent. In the following sections, we will consider affective issues such as interest, enthusiasm, and problem solving, and how each of these may help you and your

> I think it is tremendously important for parents to encourage their children's interests in mathematics, at least as much as they would encourage a star athlete. It can be hard to deal with the social stigma of being a "brain," and gifted kids really need to be comfortable enough with themselves, and confident enough to just be themselves regardless of what others think. A strong family environment is crucial to building that kind of self-confidence.
> —University Student

child's teacher in providing a fuller understanding your child's mathematically ability.

A Child's Interest in Mathematics

Mathematical ability is distinct from interest. A student does not need to be overly interested in a topic to be considered advanced in that area. As previously mentioned, many children and adults underachieve for a variety of reasons. They may have the talent and understanding to perform at advanced levels, but lack the interest to pursue continued study and investigation of the topic.

Occasionally, we find that a child may be quite talented in mathematics, but not really very interested in it. Children who are advanced in many different areas may show a definite preference for one subject or another. Additionally, what your child prefers one year may be at the bottom of his preference list the next year. Of course, enthusiasm and interest go far in motivating students toward learning success, and both are necessary if your child is expected to pursue his studies independently.

Therefore, you and your child's teacher cannot evaluate how advanced your child may be in respect to mathematics based solely upon his level of interest, or lack of interest, in the subject. Unfortunately,

> Although I had been identified as exceptionally gifted in mathematics and accelerated throughout my school years, I actually detested math for most of my time in high school. I loved to work on projects . . . stuff that could loosely be called engineering or physics. If it launched something, had to hold a weight, go a certain speed, or just plain had to be built, I was your man for the job. It is unfortunate that nobody told me that I could probably have done all of this better if I had applied some of the math I had learned in other classes.
> —University Student

a child's lack of interest often negatively affects all other measures of mathematical ability. If a child is simply not interested in mathematics, he may not give his best efforts in completing daily work or tests.

The issue of interest has a serious impact on the mathematical experiences of your child. All too often, students encounter mathematics within their K–12 educational experiences that they find to be boring. While mathematicians and mathematics educators often see the innate beauty in mathematics and think that it is really interesting, students rarely share this feeling. Additionally, traditional K–12 mathematics topics may not be challenging enough to be interesting for many mathematically talented students. Even more discouraging is the fact that potentially interesting mathematics can be taught in ways that your child finds uninteresting.

Students rarely see the ways mathematics can directly affect their lives. Your child may not see how mathematics is interconnected with some of his other interests. So, although your child may find math to be very easy, he may not be interested in actually studying it.

On the other hand, you need to know that if your child is very interested in mathematics, this is not a definite indication that she is mathematically advanced. Occasionally an average or below average student has positive feelings about mathematics. He may like it as a topic, or she may harbor no fears toward it. In either case, liking and being interested in mathematics is not the same as being advanced in math.

> Just because math is easy doesn't mean it interests me. I know that some of the students (and maybe my teachers, too) are jealous of my ability in math. I would rather be studying other things like history, but I will probably end up going for a career in math because I can earn more money.
> —Student

Playing With Mathematical Ideas

We often see students who really enjoy playing with mathematical ideas, and of course, mathematical puzzles and games entertain people of all ages. Some of these people would say that the excitement of the challenge of the puzzle is more important than the mathematics, but it is clear that they are using and enjoying math all the same. Teachers have seen many students who enjoy the challenge of solving math problems. These students take pleasure in being able to solve an equation because they see each problem as a new challenge to overcome. In essence, they compete against themselves.

> I never did any homework that did not have to be turned in. Rather, I would analyze each problem and see if I could find the "trick" to solving it. When I could find the trick, I knew I could do the rest of the problem and wouldn't bother to finish it. It was fun to see if I could outsmart the problems. —Student

You may be surprised to learn that success with many video games requires mathematical planning and the challenge of creatively balancing a number of variables. Without even realizing it, your child must perform amazingly sophisticated mathematical calculations while playing video games. Some students who claim to dislike mathematics find pleasure in computer programming, a skill that also requires mathematical understanding. Interestingly, the degree to which a person is willing to use mathematics is more often a factor of how well mathematics is camouflaged within the experience.

Nevertheless, students who involve themselves with mathematical recreations do not necessarily do so because they are mathematically talented. However, students who naturally find mathematics an easy subject to learn may be more apt to use it as a recreational medium. As with interest, enjoyment in mathematics cannot be seen as the single and most important indicator for mathematical ability, but as one piece of a very intricate puzzle.

Unusual Problem-Solving Techniques

Mathematics teachers occasionally come across the rare student who demonstrates truly unusual problem-solving techniques. These techniques are often so unusual that they can even take the teacher by surprise. Your child's teacher may report that he or she is impressed with the creative ways in which your child views a problem and finds the solution. However, this ability is often not demonstrated on the typical tests used to evaluate mathematical talent, because the design of the test forces its taker to process questions and answers in specific and predictable ways.

While the entire educational system is built upon the foundation of academic testing, this alone cannot be the sole indicator for mathematical giftedness. Nor can interest, amusement, or unconventional problem-solving strategies alone be used to determine mathematical talent. The mathematical advancement of a child can only be determined through multiple assessment strategies that paint a complete picture of the child. You will need to work closely with your local school district to create a well-rounded assessment of your child's mathematical ability.

While my class would ponder a problem, Mary would ask the most bizarre questions. Her questions usually mystified the other students and confused them. Her entire thought process differed significantly from those of the other students. If I had not had some experience with gifted students, I would have probably assumed that she did not understand what we were discussing. However, she did understand, and her questions were often much more advanced than what we were considering. —University Faculty Member

Girls and Math

It is important for parents to realize that nearly every recommendation provided in this book is appropriate for both genders. The recommendations provided here for girls assume that girls often socialize differently from boys and that our culture is not as supportive of girls in mathematical pursuits and professions at it is of boys. Thus, in this small section, we provide to parents some additional recommendations to help support the mathematical pursuits of girls.

Unfortunately, our society does a great disservice to girls who are talented in math. Although the research shows that females can be equally talented in math as males, our culture still gives girls an early message that says that they should not really be good in math and that it is best for them to pretend that they are not interested in it. Consequently, girls often do not receive the encouragement to pursue mathematics, and they seem to be exposed to far less math than boys. The outcome of this cultural bias is that if you have a daughter who is talented in math, she may find that she is the only girl in the group who chooses to pursue mathematical studies. This situation will require you to be especially supportive of your daughter so that she gets the message from you that girls can and should like math.

Some researchers have demonstrated that girls develop socially more quickly than do boys. Relationships and social interaction are more highly valued among girls than boys. Therefore, girls will be more apt to continue studies in mathematics when activities and experiences around the mathematics involve social interaction. The relationships that girls form with other girls and with female tutors, mentors, and professionals will significantly affect the degree to which they continue to be involved with mathematics. In short, the academic discipline, whether mathematics or some other field, can be valued as a conduit through which relationships with likeminded girls can be developed. Nevertheless, although the relationships they build may seem more important to girls than the actual mathematics they are studying, the outcome remains that these girls can progress much further in math through strong, supportive relationships, rather than in isolation.

Girls should be introduced to adult female role models. Introducing your daughter to female mathematicians and women in careers with a heavy emphasis in math can be helpful. In addition, you may want to provide biographies of famous women who have excelled in math. Girls need to see that entering the field of mathematics is acceptable and that many women are successful in mathematically oriented professions. Socially constructed biases against women in mathematical and scientific fields should be discussed and falsified.

In addition to introducing girls to women in the sciences, girls must be introduced to a far broader range of possible occupations that heavily utilize mathematics. With a broader understanding of the vast possibilities before them, girls will be more likely to select a career in mathematics.

Parents and teachers should encourage girls and boys into similar experiences in their pursuits of mathematics. These activities may include Advanced Placement and honors classes, mathematical competitions, tutoring, mentoring, summer camps, and countless other experiences listed elsewhere in this book. However, in doing so, parents must be continually aware that girls interact very differently within mixed gendered groups than within groups of girls alone. Parents will want to know how competition with boys affects their daughters. Some girls hold back when competing with boys and hide the full extent of their talents and understanding. Unfortunately, this often leads to them not experiencing learning as fully as those who unabashedly pursue their studies and are not intimidated with competition.

Parents must continually understand the makeup of their child and must select mathematical experiences commensurate with the child's personality, interests, and goals. Although additional social dimensions must be considered for girls, the basic principles remain.

Summary of Key Points

- A comprehensive assessment of the child's mathematical ability and achievement is necessary before beginning to plan an educational program.
- Achievement tests, ability tests, informal assessments, above-level testing, parent and teacher observations, and interest inventories all may be used in an assessment.
- Talent searches administer above-level tests for children who hit the ceiling on grade-level achievement tests.
- Although students may be advanced in math, they may not really be interested in it.
- Interest in math, enjoyment of mathematical puzzles and games, and unusual problem-solving techniques are indicators of mathematical ability, but are only part of a comprehensive assessment.
- Girls may be equally talented in mathematics as boys, but often are discouraged from advanced study of math.

Questions to Ask the School:

- What tests are you using to evaluate whether my child is advanced?
- How many times is a student tested?

- Do you use external evaluators, or are all evaluations performed in-house?
- Does the school/district use informal assessments in addition to formal assessments?

Questions to Ask the Teacher:

- How does my child's performance in math compare with his classmates?
- Do you think my child needs more challenge in his daily math lessons?
- Does my child seem to finish his work early?
- Can you please initiate testing of my child?
- Does the school offer above-level testing in math?
- Have you received training in teaching children who are mathematically advanced?
- Does my child seem to be interested in math?

Chapter 2

Navigating the School System in Support of Your Mathematically Advanced Child

s a concerned parent, you will need to interact with your child's school and seek the additional resources your child needs and deserves. In this chapter we will discuss:

- how you should interact with schools,
- what you can and should request for your child, and
- what situations you should avoid.

In addition, we will explore several of the most important types of modifications that may be made to a school's regular curriculum so that the mathematically talented child's needs may be met. These modifications include:

- compacting of the curriculum,
- acceleration by early entrance or grade skipping,

- acceleration by placement in a higher grade level for one or more subjects, and
- enrichment options.

We will also discuss ways you should prepare for meetings with school personnel and how those meetings can result in enhanced understandings and an appropriate program of study for your child. As you read through this chapter, you may want to keep in mind the contents of Table 4, "Ideas for Parents of Gifted Children to Remember."

It is essential for you to be involved with your child's school. You know your child best, and will want to make sure not only that he receives an appropriately challenging program of study but also that he grows to love learning and enjoy his mathematical interest and talent. This involvement with the school does not need to be difficult or adversarial. In fact, you should always strive to develop and maintain a congenial partnership with the school that keeps your child's best interests squarely in view.

It is important for you to realize that school budgets are already stretched to their limits. Teachers are overworked and in short supply. It may not be easy for you to convince the school that your child both needs and deserves a different curriculum, different instruction, and different tasks than average students. Nevertheless, armed with concern for your child and some understanding of state and national standards, you should be able to gently convince school

> Though my parents were never really able to help me with my math homework, they have always been encouraging and supportive of my education. They did whatever possible to make sure that I had the best education they could provide. I advise parents to discover, and provide to their children, the best available resources, including teachers and tutors.
> —University Student

Table 4.
Ideas for Parents of Gifted Children to Remember

- You are not alone. Help and information is available to assist you in understanding your gifted child's educational needs.
- Your child deserves to encounter interesting and challenging material every day.
- Gifted children should not be expected to march in place and wait for their classmates to catch up.
- Gifted children should not be asked to spend large amounts of their instructional time tutoring or helping fellow students.
- Gifted learners often acquire knowledge and skills at a faster pace than the average learner, therefore the pacing of instruction is important.
- Acceleration is an effective curricular intervention, but it is not always appropriate for every child.
- Your child's academic needs will change often.
- Your mathematically gifted child may or may not be gifted in other subject areas.
- Your mathematically gifted child may or may not be especially interested in mathematics.
- Your mathematically gifted child may need a variety of modifications, including acceleration, enrichment, or both.

---

personnel to provide your child with appropriate curricular modifications.

There is much talk in books and on the Internet encouraging you to be your child's advocate and "fight for your child's rights." As with most relationships, more can be accomplished with a team approach. Parents and school personnel should view themselves and each other as being on the same team with the shared goal of determining the best educational decisions for the child. School personnel should welcome parental input, and you should welcome the educational expertise and experience of school personnel. It will help if you can remember that the vast majority of teachers and school administrators entered the field of teaching because they truly enjoyed working with children and wanted to help them to learn. When roadblocks occur, teachers and administrators may be as unhappy and frustrated as you are about the situation, although they may not be able to tell this to you.

It is certainly true that you should advocate for your child while he is too young and inexperienced to participate fully in educational decisions. However, whenever possible, your child should also have a voice in some of the educational decision making. For example, your child will need to provide you with specific information regarding the difficulty level of his schoolwork. This means that you will need to know a bit more from your child than just "I'm bored." You will need to consult with your youngster regarding many things regarding the school such as:

- Is there too much repetition and practice of basic skills?
- Does the teacher provide too much time to complete a task?
- Are you allowed to read or work on other tasks while waiting for others to finish?
- What are the best parts of the day?
- What would help you to learn better?

An interesting and sometimes frustrating facet of public school systems is that a particular child may receive a wonderful education in one school, but the same child would receive a very inappropriate and unsatisfactory education in another school. This is partly true because the legal requirements regarding education vary greatly from state to state. State requirements are then interpreted differently from district to district and implemented differently from school to school and even from classroom to classroom. A great deal of the variance occurs because of different philosophies regarding gifted education; however, as you might expect, much of the variability is due simply to the availability of resources.

Because children are not all the same, a program that would be wonderful for one child might be ineffective and insufficient for another. Some schools do a superb job of meeting the needs of advanced children in one specific subject area, but not in others. If your child's educational strengths lie in a direction that is not well-supported, you will need to work with the school to develop a plan to support your child in that area or areas. Your role will be to assist the school personnel in understanding your child's educational strengths and needs, and help them develop a program that will be appropriately challenging and interesting so that your child will learn every day.

Underlying all of the ideas related to the modification of a school's curriculum is that curriculum is developed to meet the educational needs of the average learner in each school. The child whose needs differ from that of the average learner will require modifications that are commensurate with the degree of difference. In other words, if a child is mildly talented in mathematics, he may only need enrichment and perhaps a bit of acceleration, but if he is significantly talented in mathematics, he may need much greater acceleration and curricular modification, as well as more enrichment opportunities.

In my very first conference with my son's kindergarten teacher, she told me, "I have 25 children who come to me in September and they are performing at all different levels. My job is to hand them over to the first grade teacher in June all performing at the same level." I knew we were in trouble there, since my son already knew most of what she wanted to teach him that year. The teacher had no idea that we had a fundamental disagreement regarding a child's need to be able to learn each day.
—Parent

As discussed in Chapter 1, you and the school personnel will use the information gained through the comprehensive educational assessment to craft a program of study in mathematics that will allow your child to learn mathematical concepts and skills at an appropriate level and pace. Many parents are unsure where to begin the discussion of modification of the mathematics program. Parents ask, "If we are to be advocates, what should we be asking for?" Most parents have not pursued education as their life's work, so they sometimes feel a bit intimidated or even inadequately prepared to participate in a meeting with educational experts. By using this book and others, talking with other parents of talented children, attending conferences and presentations dealing with gifted education, and communicating with school personnel, you will develop confidence and an understanding of the school system. Don't expect to know everything before you begin working with the schools.

It is important to note that this book is not intended as a criticism of the entire public school system. There are so many excellent schools and districts that have gone to great lengths to meet the needs of all learners, and a number of schools have created excellent programs to meet the needs of mathematically advanced students. Some of these schools have specifically acted on the Gifted Program Standards, previously discussed in the introduction, in order to address these concerns. These schools and programs should be applauded for their efforts and should be emulated by other schools that have yet to adequately meet the learning needs of mathematically advanced students.

Some schools have gifted programs that are well-integrated within the school system. Others have school personnel who are specifically trained to work with mathematically advanced students. Some may have excellent avenues of communication with parents and some schools have already made connections with mathematics experts and university faculty. The best schools are willing to make positive changes on a yearly basis as determined by the needs of the students.

Sensitivity to the School System

As you begin to think about how to interact with your child's school to seek the support and resources needed for your mathematically advanced child, it is important to remember how very busy teachers and administrators are. Your sensitivity to the burden already set upon the system and individual personnel is essential for open communication and effective collaboration between parents and school personnel. Parents must remember that hundreds of students attend each school, and many students are in need of additional resources in order to simply meet minimum competencies.

Of course, most teachers teach many different subjects or courses throughout the entire day and perform countless other duties in the school, and adding meetings and paperwork to an already very busy schedule can be very difficult. Additional resources, support, personnel, and supplies all have costs associated with them, and schools and districts have limited funds at their disposal. Partially because of these budgetary limits, some schools are usually not quick to provide services to small groups of students, particularly when the services cannot be provided to all students.

However, although schools may already seem overburdened with responsibilities and services that they are already expected to deliver, the school's burdens cannot supersede your concern for your child. Nor does any overwhelming pressure on schools

---

Preparing for the Conference

- Gather and review all of the paperwork that you have received regarding any testing and evaluations that have been done.
- Talk with your child so that you have a clear idea of her perspective of the current academic program.
- Decide your goals for the conference.
- Decide on educationally reasonable requests that you can suggest.
- Invite someone who is familiar with gifted education and mathematics to accompany you to the conference, if you wish.
- Take your child's work samples and supporting materials to the conference.
- Try to be sure that both parents attend the conference, if at all possible.

---

lessen the responsibility of the school to meet the academic needs of the gifted learner. This creates a fine line on which both schools and parents must walk; parents' understanding of the school's atmosphere and responsibilities is essential.

Bright children have the same right as all other children to learn something new every day. They should not be required to march in place while waiting for their classmates to catch up to them. Nor should they repeatedly be asked to use their instructional time in school to tutor or help their less able classmates instead of making progress on their understanding of important content. Unfortunately, many teachers are overwhelmed by large classes filled with children who are learning at various achievement levels. For example, a third-grade teacher may have children in her class who have not yet learned to read at all, and she could also have one or even two children who can read on the college level.

> In kindergarten, our school district discouraged us from having our son tested because of his age and we listened (bad choice on our part!). They finally initiated testing in first grade and he scored above the 99.9% in math. Other than when he is pulled out of regular class for gifted enrichment, he is extremely bored.—Parent

Given this situation, a busy teacher may believe that her time should be spent helping the children who are working below grade level and struggling with daily work, instead of assisting children who came to the class already knowing the grade-level content. Your academically advanced child may be achieving several grade levels above her placement, and some teachers would be content to allow her to simply complete the assigned work and perhaps even provide help to some of her classmates who are in need of assistance.

Administrators may have similar ideas regarding the educational needs of mathematically advanced children. In addition, administrators are often concerned about the resources that may be needed in order to offer any modification to instruction for these children. If a program is offered for one child, administrators must be prepared to offer the same program to all other children who have similar needs. Sadly, some administrators recognize that you, as the parent of advanced child, may find it very difficult to advocate for your child. In fact, many parents will eventually give up and go away. This is part of the reason you might have difficulty getting some administrators' attention and cooperation.

As advocates for gifted education, we have often seen teachers who want to provide the necessary modifications to the curriculum for mathematically gifted children, but are afraid to do so unless directed to by the administration. You will need to work with administrators so that your child's teacher will be given the opportunity to design a program and deliver it without fear of reprisal from the district administration.

What the Law Says About Gifted Children

In order to make sure your mathematically advanced child receives the education he deserves, it is important to understand a little of the background regarding the way in which the education of talented children has evolved in the United States. With this understanding, you will be able to gain a greater knowledge of the concept of giftedness and how it works. In turn, you will be able to advocate more effectively for your child if that should be become necessary. Although your child may or may not be identified as gifted, it can be very helpful for you to understand the provisions in the laws that apply to gifted children.

Although there is no federal mandate requiring that schools provide special programs for gifted children, the federal law No Child Left Behind (NCLB; 2001) addresses teaching quality and professional development. According to NCLB, teachers must be provided with in-service training that addresses the topics of different learning styles, special learning needs, and instructional strategies to teach gifted and high performing children. In addition, the Gifted Program Standards (discussed in the Introduction of this book) devote an entire section to professional development in an effort to ensure that personnel who work with gifted children are well-trained and supported.

In 1993, the U.S. Department of Education published its report, *National Excellence: A Case for Developing America's Talent.* Among other things, the report provided an updated definition of gifted learners that is frequently used. Gifted learners, the report says, are children with potential or demonstrated exceptional talents significantly higher than the potential or demonstrated accomplishments of their peers (U.S. Department of Education).

> Our school asked if they could administer psychological tests and out-of-level achievement tests to our son. After the testing, we were invited to work with the school to make an educational plan for him, since he was gifted in mathematics. He was accelerated one grade level in mathematics and he also participated in math enrichment activities. —Parent

Some states have no special provisions for gifted children in their educational regulations. However, other states have developed extensive regulations that describe the requirements of gifted education. For example, the state of Pennsylvania has made a commitment to gifted students as "children with exceptionalities" who are in need of specially designed instruction. Indeed, the definition of mentally gifted used in Pennsylvania is someone with outstanding creative and intellectual ability. The definition also notes that this ability requires specially designed programs or support services (or both) that are not ordinarily provided in the regular classroom. Identification may not be based on an IQ score alone, but a 130 or higher IQ score is one indication of giftedness. Schools are required to use multiple criteria when attempting to identify gifted children, including (but not limited to) achievement test scores, acquisition and retention rates, demonstrated achievement, and performance or expertise in one or more academic areas. Perhaps not surprisingly, although some state mandates regulate the education of gifted children, these mandates are often implemented differently by local educational agencies. Thus, a gifted child might receive a very different education based on the philosophy and funding currently in place in the school district and state in which he resides.

If you find that you need to know more about the legal issues surrounding gifted education in your state, you should contact your state's Department of Education for further information. In addition, there are three books that are helpful in this area, all written by Frances Karnes and Ronald Marquardt. *Gifted Children and the Law: Mediation, Due Process, and Court Cases* (1991a), *Gifted Children and Legal Issues in Education: Parents' Stories of Hope* (1991b), and *Gifted Children and Legal Issues in Education: An Update* (2000) all provide resource information and background regarding cases that have been settled in the courts. You should be sure to make every effort to work with a school before resorting to legal measures, because a court battle can be both emotionally and financially costly.

One of the best places for you to gain information regarding legal and advocacy issues is through a parent group. The resources section of this book lists the addresses and Web sites for many organizations for gifted education, and it is very important for you to connect with one or more of these. If there is a local parent group, just attending the meetings and finding parents who have similar concerns can go a long way. If no such group exists, you may wish to explore creating one. Often a teacher or professor at a local college or university will assist in such efforts. Additionally, state affiliates of the National Association for Gifted Children will often assist in getting a local gifted advisory group up and running.

Joining an online electronic mailing list can also be beneficial, because many parents have had similar questions and are willing to share their experiences with you. In addition to their printed materials and Web sites, national and state organizations host conferences and annual meetings, and parents are welcome to attend. A thorough understanding of giftedness or advanced mathematical ability will enhance your ability to nurture your child's talent.

> When I was placed in a class with other mathematically gifted children, I learned about the legal battle that my parents had been waging with the school district. Previously, the acceleration and enrichment I had received had benefitted only myself, but now the school district was forced to create a math class for all mathematically gifted children. I learned two things: There were many other children that were as talented as I without parents who were able to fight for their education, and that the efforts of one or two concerned parents could improve the quality of education for an entire school district. —Student

What Schools Should Avoid Doing
for/to the Mathematically Advanced Child

Parents of a mathematically talented child must protect him or her from scenarios that often occur within the public schools. Four specific concerns immediately face parents of the mathematically advanced child. These concerns may be identified by the following situations:

- more of the same work, piled higher,
- using students as teachers or tutors,
- every child gets the same work, and
- topical redundancy in a subject area.

Although more areas of concern certainly exist, these often seem to be the most problematic, and you must be aware of them.

More, Piled Higher

In an effort to provide for them, teachers sometimes bombard advanced students with a huge amount of homework and assignments. High school and university honors programs are notorious for burdening students with an almost indecent workload. In many cases, the additional assignments given to many advanced students are little more than busy work. They often fail to press students into deeper thought, but simply take a great deal of time to complete.

I knew a child in a university honors program who was so burdened by a heavy workload that she eventually dropped out of the honors program and almost out of college altogether. The "honors" component of the program seemed to have more to do with volume [of work] than anything else. Being a student in that honors program was something of a race of endurance; students who could endure the brutal pace were deemed competent. —High School Teacher

We call this instructional methodology *more of the same, piled higher*. In some cases, the *more* is piled so high that it makes the program educationally unsound.

The more of the same, piled higher mentality is often seen with well-meaning educators who are inadequately trained regarding curriculum modification for advanced students. Teachers often mistake doing more work for deeper and broader investigations. This is a shame; nevertheless, it is also a reality.

You may find that your advanced student is overloaded with class work once it is noted that she is advanced. When this happens, you will need to intervene and protect your child from this burden. Many advanced students are very frustrated with receiving much more work than their classmates, and they may become discouraged about the entire educational system. Educators regularly see the very brightest students drop out of school and choose employment and lifestyles vastly below their potential.

If you believe that your child is receiving assignments that mainly waste his time, you should certainly talk with the teacher about the situation. You and your child may need to make some difficult decisions. You may even need to pull your child out of advanced programs that are inappropriate if the school personnel persist in requiring too much repetitious work. Notably, in so doing, you may also be taking your child out of the only program in the school with the potential to meet her advanced academic needs. Nevertheless, there are many ways in which programs fail to meet the needs of advanced students, and the more, piled higher paradigm can be as great a disservice as not having any advanced programs. Conversely, there are also many means independent of the public school system by which to meet the needs of the advanced student. These are addressed in upcoming chapters.

Using Students as Teachers or Tutors

It is important for you to take a firm position that your child is a student and not a teacher. All too often, advanced students are used as classroom tutors for other students. Teachers who are overburdened by oversized classes and by the academic struggles of other students sometimes ask the advanced student to go to various desks and tables and tutor struggling students. Due to the fact that so few students are mathematically proficient, and that mathematics teachers are elated with even the slightest assistance in their classrooms, using talented students as tutors may occur more frequently in mathematics than in many other subjects.

Using students as classroom tutors is an unethical alternative to providing your child with the additional academic resources she needs. It is the responsibility of teachers and the entire school system to educate all students, including your mathematically advanced child. Some educators could argue that students learn more when they teach material to others, and when they practice communicating their understanding of this material to others. With this, few educators would disagree. However, you need to ask a teacher who uses her talented student as a tutor if she requires all students to take a turn tutoring other classmates, or what other educational opportunities she offers to her talented students. The teacher can be asked how she modifies the pace, depth, and breadth of the curriculum for the student she uses as a tutor. All too often, using talented students as tutors will be the only enrichment experience provided to mathematically advanced students. This simply cannot continue.

> I was in fifth grade when I decided to become a teacher. After all, that is what I was doing all day—tutoring my classmates. I didn't mind it then, but later I got tired of being called the teacher's pet and never getting to learn anything.
> —Gifted Student

While you really must protect your child from becoming a class tutor, you should not dismiss this possibility altogether, because the experience of tutoring can be extremely valuable. It is only when tutoring is used as a replacement for other experiences that it becomes problematic. The best plan is for you to be adequately involved with your child's teachers so you can find an appropriate balance in your child's experiences.

Every Child Gets the Same

Equity is a fundamental principle within much of education today. Unfortunately, many people still misunderstand the meaning of equity. Equity does *not* mean that everyone gets the same thing: resources, teaching, homework, texts, and assignments; that expectations for each student are exactly alike; or that what one child gets, all children get. Rather, equity means that each child gets what he or she needs to flourish academically. Some students will need certain resources and experiences to fully meet their mathematical potential; others will need an entirely different set of resources and experiences.

> My list of "Thou Shalt Nots" for a school district, would be brief. "Thou shalt not hold kids back" would really just about cover everything. Wouldn't it be nice if children could learn at their own rate, not necessarily the rate of the kid beside them on the bus, not the statistically average rate, but one that is all their own? —Gifted Student

You will need to ensure that your child is getting the educational resources she needs. This is especially important for children participating in programs for advanced students. Even though your child may be surrounded by other bright students, appropriate resources, and rich educational experiences, one size does not fit all. So, whatever educational setting your child is in, it may not be the most effective to fulfill her educational needs.

In order for you to be sure that your child's unique needs are met, it is important for you to know your own child well and have a very open line of communication with him. You need to know his opinion of the value of his academic experiences. You simply need to know what is working and not working for him. Additionally, you should be sure to have open lines of communication with your child's school and teachers.

Topical Redundancy

Most mathematics students in U.S. schools suffer through years of topical redundancy, which is the repetition of particular units of study in mathematics. This often leads to mathematical boredom and crippling disinterest. Much of the entire K–12 mathematics curriculum is built on an ever expanding spiral of both new and recycled ideas. Unfortunately, the number of mathematical concepts that are annually rehashed seems to far exceed the number of new ideas provided for students to contemplate. If this instills a sense of boredom and disinterest for average students, it is often all the more so for talented students. Average students may need to repeatedly see mathematical concepts in order to fully comprehend them. However, advanced students often grasp a concept with only a few repetitions, so topical redundancy can be more debilitating to advanced students than to others.

Again, the primary means by which you can be involved in protecting your child from topical redundancy is similar to that of previously mentioned concerns; you must communicate openly with school personnel to develop a strong and healthy academic plan for your mathematically advanced student.

Common Topics in Math Classrooms

Parents are often unsure about what topics are covered in which grades and mathematics courses, and many are surprised to find how difficult this question is to answer even by a professional mathematics educator. Although the National Council of Teachers of Mathematics (NCTM) has produced recommended national standards, each state modifies NCTM's recommendations as they see fit. Then, school districts further modify state suggested standards. Therefore, it is impossible to find exact standards shared by all schools. Furthermore, NCTM's recommendations are made in respect to grade bands and not specific grades or courses. Thus, states and districts are free to change NCTM's recommendations as desired.

However, although there is no absolute rule as to what topics are covered in mathematics at each grade, an adequate number of commonalities exist to guide those who are interested. The following list (see Table 5) has been generated from NCTM's recommendations, along with the recommendations of no less than eight states. These recommendations are more general and might lack the specificity that you may desire. Nevertheless, they are useful if you would like to determine what your child should be learning in his current grade or classroom.

Table 5 presents a list of the common topics covered in math classes. You should not feel intimidated if you don't know what many of the terms mean. Consultation with a public school or university mathematics educator should quickly provide answers to any questions you may have. This list can be used to communicate with schools systems, teachers, and tutors. Notably, some of the items on the list are skills and others are goals for understanding.

Methods for Differentiation of the Curriculum for Advanced Students

For children who are very advanced in mathematics, acceleration is the most effective curricular intervention. However, many parents, teachers, and administrators fear acceleration of any kind, and think that it will harm the child in some way. Many years of research have provided us with conclusive evidence that appropriate acceleration is a very positive and educationally sound way of meeting the needs of some children. This is not to say that acceleration is the proper solution for every child. It is important to remember that along with the comprehensive educational evaluation discussed earlier, several other factors need to be examined, including the child's social and emotional development, the child's attitude toward the proposed acceleration, and the attitude of the school personnel who will be involved with the child.

For example, a 10-year-old in fifth grade has been determined by careful diagnostic testing to be ready to learn mathematical content and skills that are usually presented to seventh graders. Eric learns mathematics easily and quickly, often needing little repetition to attain mastery of the content and skills. Is there any reason why we would force this fifth grader to wait for 2 years before allowing him to learn the mathematics material for which he is now ready? Is this really accelerating a child if we are simply placing him correctly within the curricular sequence and allowing him to move ahead? What would be the best way to meet Eric's need for advanced mathematical material that is provided at an appropriate pace?

There are many types of acceleration, and these may be grouped into four main categories:
- early admission and grade skipping,
- compacting material within a grade level,

Table 5
Common Topics Covered in Mathematics Classrooms

Students in grades Pre-K–2 should be able to:
- count the number of objects and understand magnitude of whole numbers;
- understand base-10 place value and be able to decompose and compare numbers;
- understand basic fractions;
- understand and compute addition and subtraction of whole numbers;
- begin understanding of multiplication and division;
- sort, classify, and order objects;
- recognize, describe, and extend geometric and arithmetic patterns;
- begin to understand principles and properties of operations and relations;
- use multiple representations leading to the symbolic;
- analyze and describe qualitative change;
- describe and compare attributes and parts of two- and three-dimensional shapes;
- describe and interpret positions in space and interpret direction and distance;
- apply simple geometric transformations and symmetry;
- relate geometry to number and measurement;
- recognize and compare objects by length, volume, weight, area, and time;
- measure using nonstandard and standard units;
- pose questions, gather data, represent data using multiple representations, and describe what the data demonstrates; and
- develop an understanding of likely and unlikely events.

Students in grades 3–5 should be able to:
- understand the base-10 place value system in respect to decimals;
- use multiple representations for equivalent numbers and understand fractions, decimals, and percents and their magnitudes;
- begin to use negative numbers;
- determine factors and multiples of natural numbers;
- understand and compute multiplication and division of whole numbers;
- understand the use of inverse operations and properties of operations and relations;

- use multiple representations to begin understanding of computations involving fractions and decimals;
- use multiple representation to analyze, describe, extend, and make generalizations about patterns and functions;
- begin to use variables (letters and symbols) and develop equations;
- begin to investigate multiple types of variables and how variables in equations relate;
- use the concepts of congruence and similarity;
- begin reasoning and informal proofs about geometric properties and relationships;
- describe location, movement, and distance on coordinate systems;
- use multiple transformations and rotational symmetry on geometric figures;
- convert from one unit of measurement to another in a system;
- estimate perimeters, areas, and volumes of irregular shapes and understand relationships between perimeter and area;
- develop and use formulas to find the area and volume of geometric figures;
- investigate data-collection methods;
- use multiple representations to depict data and relationships and describe distributions;
- use measures of central tendency;
- design studies and propose and justify conclusions and predictions; and
- understand events as certain, equally likely, and impossible and predict outcomes of simple experiments.

Students in grades 6–8 should be able to:
- understand and compute fluently with fractions, decimals, and percents;
- understand and use ratios and proportions;
- understand and use scientific notation for very large and very small numbers;
- understand factors, multiples, prime factorization, and relatively prime numbers;
- understand and use integers;
- use multiple representations to investigate and apply linear and nonlinear functions;
- in respect to change, explain the meaning of intercept and slope of a line;

Table 6, continued

- use multiple representations and symbolic algebra to represent situations and relationships;
- rewrite algebraic expressions into equivalent forms and solve linear equations;
- understand and use relationships among geometric figures and their parts and use inductive and deductive arguments regarding these relationships;
- use coordinate geometry to investigate geometric shapes;
- use geometric properties to construct geometric objects;
- connect geometry, number, and algebra to explain concepts in the other domain and to real-world investigations;
- use the metric system;
- extend the use of formulas to circles and other quadrilaterals and then to more complex two- and three-dimensional shapes;
- investigate velocity and density;
- using multiple representations, appropriate graphical representations, and lines of best fit, investigate, compare, and make conjectures regarding data from two populations;
- determine and use measures of central tendency and dispersion;
- understand complementary and mutually exclusive events;
- using proportions, make and test probabilistic conjectures; and
- use organized lists, tree diagrams, and area models to compute probabilities.

Students in grades 9–12 should be able to:
- understand, compute, and use the properties of operations, relations, and roots of polynomials in various number systems and mathematical systems (vectors and matrices);
- use number-theory arguments to study whole numbers;
- use permutations and combinations;
- define functions explicitly and recursively;
- understand relations and functions through multiple representations;
- investigate rates of change, intercepts, zeros, and asymptotic behavior of functions of one variable;
- understand and use algebraic transformations by hand and with technology;

- understand and apply the properties of classes of functions (exponential, polynomial, rational, logarithmic, and periodic functions);
- understand representations of functions of two variables;
- understand and use equivalent forms of expressions, equations, inequalities, and relations;
- use functions and symbolic expressions to model quantitative relationships;
- interpret rates of change from various representations;
- prove geometric theorems;
- use trigonometry to calculate lengths and angle measures;
- use various coordinate systems (Cartesian, polar, and spherical systems);
- use sketches, coordinates, vectors, function notation, and matrices to perform transformations;
- draw and construct geometric figures using a variety of tools;
- apply graph theory to appropriate problems;
- analyze and apply concepts of precision, accuracy, approximate error, successive approximation, upper and lower bounds, and limit in measurement;
- make appropriate inferences from various models of studies;
- design studies and understand randomization, categorical data, and univariate and bivariate data;
- as appropriate for univariate and bivariate data, properly display the distribution or relationship, calculate summary statistics, and determine regression equations and correlation coefficients using technological tools;
- use simulations for sample statistics and construct sampling distributions;
- infer sample statistics to population parameters;
- design studies;
- construct sample spaces and distributions;
- use simulations to construct and investigate empirical probability distributions;
- compute and interpret the expected values; and
- use conditional probability techniques and compute the probability of compound events.

- continuous progress or self-paced instruction, and
- mentoring and extracurricular programs.

Each category has pros and cons regarding the delivery and suitability of each type of acceleration for any particular child. You will need to work closely with educational personnel in order to determine which type of acceleration would be best suited for your child. In fact, as your child matures, the optimal type of accelerative option may change for her, based on social and emotional factors and pragmatic considerations such as travel and grouping options.

Early admission is an accelerative option that refers to a child entering kindergarten, middle school, high school, or college earlier than his agemates. This placement allows for a better match between the child and the curriculum. It is best reserved for children who are generally advanced in most subject areas. *Grade skipping* is closely related to early admission, and can be implemented for a child who is academically, socially, and emotionally ready to interact with children who are a grade level ahead.

> When I was in third grade, I went to the fourth grade just for math. By fifth grade, I skipped again and took math with accelerated seventh graders. I mostly liked this, but I had to ride a special bus between schools and my school day was longer. But, it was better than being bored.
> —Student

Concerns related to early admission and grade skipping are often centered on things such as the possible negative social consequences of being younger (and perhaps smaller in stature) than classmates. You may worry about your child being unable to drive when his classmates do, and may fear that you are pushing your child to grow up too fast. Our experience is that advanced children often prefer to interact with older children or adults who share their interests. In fact, a bright child may feel rather isolated among his agemates because his abilities and interests often don't match theirs.

It is also possible for your child to skip a grade just for mathematics instruction. This is a less radical method of grade skipping that works well for children who are very strong in mathematics, but less talented in other subjects. It may be that the grade level determined by his age is fine for all subject areas except mathematics. Some children will even need to advance two grade levels in mathematics; this too can work well. However, one of the difficulties of grade skipping in a single subject is the scheduling conflict that can occur. A child who is grade skipped may also need special transportation between buildings, such as the situation when a fifth grader attends a sixth-grade math class and needs special transportation to a local middle school. A similar problem occurs between middle and high school, if the two schools are in different buildings. Even if the classes are in the same building, some scheduling conflicts can occur.

Parents (and administrators) often express concern that a child who has been accelerated in mathematics will run out of courses to take before she graduates from high school. This may happen, but that need not be the end of her progress in mathematics. Many colleges welcome high school students, and *distance learning* options are increasingly available. Some students take a math course at a local community college while they are still enrolled in high school, allowing them to earn college credit.

It is important for you to discuss and weigh all of the factors when mak-

> Parents, your should praise your children for every good grade they receive, forgive their mistakes, and, most of all, allow them to choose for themselves whether or not to take advanced math. Pushing children to do something they don't want to do will not result in progress. Perhaps next year the child will be ready to take on an advanced course.
> —University Student

ing decisions about acceleration, and experienced teachers and administrators may be helpful in this regard. In addition, you may want to talk with other parents of children who have skipped a grade or entered school early. You may want to request that the school use an instrument such as the Iowa Acceleration Scale (Assouline, Colangelo, Lupkowski-Shoplik, Lipscomb, & Forstadt, 2003) to facilitate the gathering of necessary information and assist with the decision of how much acceleration would be best for a particular child.

A less radical accelerative option than early admission or grade skipping is *compacting the curriculum* within the child's regular grade level. This is accomplished by the classroom teacher, and is especially helpful for children for whom grade skipping is not appropriate. In order to compact the curriculum, the teacher gives preassessments or pretests before each unit of study. All or only a few of the students may take the pretest. Based on the results of the pretest, the teacher will determine if a student has already mastered the material of that chapter. If a child has demonstrated that he has acquired the skills and content to be presented, he has the option of participating in alternate activities during the time that his classmates are working on the chapter. The alternate activities may be enrichment or acceleration in mathematics, and should reflect the child's interest, talent, and pace. Children who test out of classroom lessons and activities should not be asked to do more mathematical problems of the same type "just for practice."

The benefits of compacting the curriculum are:

- Students who test out of a chapter can use the time they gain to study the topic in greater depth.
- They are spared the boredom of being required to sit through lessons they don't need and doing homework that is too easy for them.

- Children who test out of similar material may be able to work together on projects of mutual interest.
- Students may not demonstrate mastery of the entire chapter, and compacting allows the flexibility for them to rejoin the class for the lessons they need.

The issues related to *grouping* students are important and deserve some explanation here. In U.S. schools, there currently is a tendency to avoid grouping students by ability, because this process is sometimes confused with tracking. In the 1980s, tracking earned a negative reputation because some research showed that students from lower groups (or tracks) often received inferior materials and instruction. Students in the higher, or more able, groups often got newer books and better teachers. In schools that used tracking, the children were usually assigned to a track and they stayed in that particular track for all of their schooling. Ability grouping, however, is not the same as tracking, and does not deserve to be shunned. In fact, grouping children by ability has been shown to be very effective in producing educational gains as long as the curriculum, materials, and classroom activities are tailored to each group. This is critical to the success of ability grouping, and it is easy to see why.

For example, imagine an elementary school that has 120 fourth-grade children in four mixed ability classrooms of 30 children. Within that group of 120 children, some will be unable to add single digits, while others will be able to understand the concepts of division and metric conversions. If the children were

Sometimes we were tested to check our level of math; we worked in small groups with other kids at our level, and the teacher worked with each group separately. The higher group worked alone a lot more than the other kids because we didn't need things explained to us as much. —Teaching Assistant, University Level regrouped by ability for mathematics, each class could contain students of more similar ability and achievement. The teachers could then match their instruction to the needs of the children in their class with more accuracy, because there would not be such a wide range of ability. The pace of instruction could be more appropriate for more of the students, and the more able students would not need to wait for the less able to catch up. A key component of ability grouping is that children are reassessed frequently and assigned to a different group when necessary. The 120 fourth graders could be grouped by ability in other subjects, too, and these groups would likely be different, because the child who is strongest in math may not also be the strongest in reading. This is known as regrouping by subject area ability.

Another grouping strategy that is helpful for children is called *cluster grouping*. This is simply ability grouping on a smaller scale. Students of similar ability are clustered together to study a particular topic in mathematics, but may rejoin the larger group for other subject areas. You may find that if your school refuses to consider ability grouping for mathematics instruction they may be willing to cluster group the advanced children so that they may receive instruction more in sync with their abilities.

> When I look back on positive educational experiences in elementary and middle schools, they are without fail in the context of some form of ability grouping. Simply put, this is where the good stuff happened! —Gifted Student

The Diagnostic Testing-Prescriptive Instruction (DT-PI) approach is much more individualized than grade skipping or compacting. The DT-PI model shares its roots with special education, and it was early researcher Leta Hollingworth who recognized that the idea of out-of-level testing could be useful with gifted students (Assouline & Lupkowski-Shoplik,

2005). However, it was Julian Stanley who extended upon Hollingworth's ideas in the 1960s and 1970s to develop the DT-PI model. Using the model, Stanley was able to identify talented math students' strengths and recognize areas where they were weak and needed more work. One component of the DT-PI model is its systematic, objective approach in determining the most appropriate curricula to use with talented math students (Assouline & Lupkowski-Shoplik).

Simply put, the teacher administers a diagnostic test to determine what content and skills the child has already mastered. An individualized plan of instruction listing topics and instructional activities to be completed is then developed. The child works at his own pace, either independently or with instruction from the teacher. Upon completion of the prescribed activities, the student is tested on the new content to see if he has mastered it. The teacher will again prescribe instruction, which may give the child a bit more work in the topic just covered or may allow him to move onto new information if he demonstrates mastery of the topic.

You can see that there are many different ways to meet your child's needs if he is ready to receive mathematics instruction at a much higher level. Choosing a solution will depend on many factors. For example, how does the school handle grade skipping of one subject area? If the teachers and administration are firmly against it, and your child would be the only one accelerated in this way, it obviously will be more difficult to convince the school to accelerate your daughter. Is your child's teacher experienced in curriculum compacting or DT-PI? Does your child prefer to work independently or with a group? These are just a few of the concerns you need to consider.

If it is possible for your child to be advanced a grade in mathematics, will he be placed with older students of average ability in mathematics or with children who are taking algebra a year before the average student? Placing your child in a mathematics class with average learners might not be the best plan, because the pace of instruction for that class will likely be too slow for him. A class for accelerated students might be a better choice because the pace of instruction will be more appropriate.

Enrichment Programs

Many schools offer enrichment programs specifically geared toward gifted children. The programs are often of the pull-out variety, whereby a child attends the enrichment program for perhaps 2 hours each week and spends the remainder of her school experience in the regular classroom. The amount of time can vary, with some schools offering a whole day in the special program. If your child has not been identified as gifted but needs to receive enrichment in mathematics that could be provided through the enrichment program that gifted children in her school receive, you should ask the school to allow your child to join the group for mathematics enrichment.

Enrichment programs may be a time for students to get together and practice for upcoming competitions. Other programs focus on the arts, and children study a play or opera they will later attend. Another type of enrichment program allows children to work on problem-solving strategies or participate in Socratic seminars to develop their reasoning and communication abilities. Some programs require students to develop projects or study teacher-

> In the enrichment class, we spent all year learning about a country and I did more activities and projects in that one year than I did in the previous two years. We went on field trips and had an International Bazaar to display our projects about the country we had studied. It was really fun.
> —Gifted Student

selected units such as foreign countries, architecture, bridges, or even holidays. For the mathematically talented child, often the best kind of enrichment program is one that allows her to study mathematics in greater depth, as well as participate in competitions. Enrichment programs are very helpful for children who need more than the regular curriculum provides but do not require acceleration.

Curricular Modification in Mathematics Education

In addition to the general accelerative options that have been discussed that work for any curricular area, there are many options specifically relevant to mathematics that will provide acceleration and enrichment for mathematically talented students. For example, mathematics is not limited to the curricula seen in most K–12 schools. Arithmetic, tech math, algebra, geometry, discrete mathematics, precalculus, statistics, and calculus are only a small subset of all mathematical topics, even those that are within the understanding of K–12 students. Mathematically advanced students are capable of learning a greater breadth of mathematical topics. Traditional curricula, without extension or modification, may bore students who learn quickly.

Although some children can perform mathematical calculations quickly without having any real understanding of the mathematics involved, other children have difficulty with basic calculations yet are very strong in their conceptual understanding. Some teachers in this situation want to force the child to practice basic calculations endlessly while holding them back from further development of their conceptual knowledge. This is a real disservice to advanced children, and can be very frustrating to them. If allowed to continue to make progress on mathematical concepts while working on more advanced problems, a child's ability to perform the basic calculations will improve over time.

Many of the mathematics textbooks currently being used in schools employ a spiral approach to the delivery of mathematics. This means that a topic is introduced in an early grade and taken a bit further in each successive grade. Children in the early grades are not expected to go into much depth with the topics, and little time and attention is given to mastery of the concepts or skills. This can be frustrating for advanced children, because if their interest is engaged in a topic, they will often want to take it as far as they can, instead of just waiting until the same topic comes around again the next year. Educators call this a linear approach, and it is often much more appropriate for advanced children than the spiral approach advocated in most textbooks.

You may wonder how to work with the school system to provide your mathematically advanced child with a broader mathematical experience than what is seen in accepted textbooks. If you are not mathematically inclined, you may feel at a loss when working with schools regarding the curriculum modifications that would benefit your child. The following ideas are presented to help you to formulate suggestions based upon what you know about your child.

Pace, Breadth, and Depth

Three dimensions of enrichment should be considered for mathematically advanced students: pace, breadth, and depth. These dimensions should not be considered independent of each other. The ability of the mathematically gifted child may determine which and how many of these dimensions should be addressed simultaneously. The duration of any curricular enrichment is also a component to be considered in respect to curricular modification. For instance, if a teacher has a student for only a few months, the teacher may be limited to what degree he or she may be able to modify the depth or breadth of the mathematical investigations done by a student. Figure 1 gives a good example of how these dimensions interrelate. In addition, Table 6 details how teachers use these dimensions in the classroom.

Modifying the Pace of Mathematics

Many advanced students are very content to simply blaze through course after course at an accelerated pace. Some may quite easily complete two or more courses in the same time that average students complete one. Some advanced students prefer to take simultaneous advanced mathematics courses; this too may fulfill the need for speed. Advanced students often grasp new information from fewer examples. Significantly advanced mathematics students can often exhaust the possibilities of courses provided at their local high school. When this occurs, you might want to consider college courses. While uncommon, high school students can occasionally be found in traditional college mathematics courses. Thus, changing the pace of mathematical investigation may occur within a course or a series of courses, and even among a number of schools.

Remaining sections in this chapter provide more detail on allowing students

> More than once, I have had high school students in my university mathematics courses. On one occasion, I even remember a student who was so young that he had to be driven to and from the university by his mother. Interestingly, these high school students were generally the best students in my courses and earned the highest grades.
> —University Mathematics Faculty Member

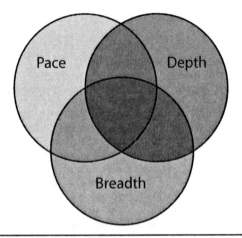

Figure 1. Pace, breadth, and depth Venn diagram

to experience mathematical studies in greater depth and breadth. The following sections demonstrate additional ways in which classroom teachers and schools can provide the educational experiences needed by mathematically advanced students. Some of these are very simple to provide to students; others are more difficult.

Modifying Breadth of Mathematics

Textbook Problems

In most textbooks, homework problems get increasingly complex throughout a given lesson or topic. They eventually extend the basic mathematical discussion into more broad mathematical realms. Thus, the problems presented near the end of a given topic naturally broaden the mathematical study. All too often, these latter problems are not assigned in regular classrooms, and advanced students do not receive the benefit of their breadth. You can make sure that your child receives the benefits of these extensions by simply ensuring that your child does the problems

Table 6
Means of Enhancing Mathematical Experiences
Through Modifying Pace, Breadth, and Depth

Pace:
- topical acceleration
- course acceleration
- grade acceleration
- covering additional topics

Breadth:
- covering additional topics
- extending investigations beyond the academic topics
- connecting mathematical concepts from one mathematical field to another
- demonstrating how mathematics integrates into students' real lives
- doing latter problems in textbooks
- reading mathematics texts
- investigating mathematics on the Internet
- emphasizing problem solving, reasoning and proof, communication, connections, and representations

Depth:
- looking at similar topics but at a higher level
- reading mathematics texts
- doing latter problems in texts
- investigating mathematics using technology
- investigating mathematics on the Internet
- examining the *hows* and *whys* of mathematics

at the end of each section. Unfortunately, however, this may create a situation where your child is required to do more homework than his regular classmates. This problem may be eliminated if the teacher will ask your child to concentrate on the latter problems rather than the former in any section of the textbook.

Reading Mathematics

Most often, the classroom emphasis is on *doing* mathematics rather than reading mathematics. Reading mathematical texts can be quite fulfilling for some advanced mathematics students. Recognizing how the author constructs mathematical ideas and provides examples can be a rewarding exercise. Your child should be encouraged to carefully read the entire text prior to attempting any homework problems. This practice, although uncommon, can greatly enhance mathematical learning.

Textbooks are not the only source of mathematical reading. Many books are written to unfold mathematical ideas on the high school and college undergraduate level, and some are written in very attractive and engaging styles. A few of these books can be purchased in traditional bookstores and college bookstores, and countless more can be found for sale on the Internet. Through this type of broad reading, topics usually undiscovered in K–12 textbooks can be developed and considered. Your child can find dozens of books to broaden her interests and understanding of mathematics and the countless applications of mathematics to real-world phenomena can be investigated.

Mathematics journals provide excellent sources of interesting, broad mathematical reading. A variety of journals are stored at nearly every K–12 school and hundreds are housed in university libraries. Journals in the fields of mathematics, science, and mathematics and science education are widely available, and advanced mathematics students should be able to easily read many of these. However, a number of mathematically specialized journals are quite advanced, and some are beyond the ability of all but the most advanced mathematicians. These more advanced journals may simultaneously stimulate your child to look more deeply into mathematics while frustrating her because of the complexity of the reading. Teachers, tutors, and mentors may also offer suggestions for additional mathematics reading material.

Multiple Textbooks

Using multiple textbooks can significantly broaden the mathematics that your child is studying, and you can usually find additional textbooks in libraries and in the mathematics department office in most schools. Universities often have numerous extra copies of older texts scattered throughout faculty offices and mathematics departments, and these usually can be borrowed for indefinite periods of time. University libraries also hold hundreds of old and new textbooks, which can often be borrowed.

It is very important that you not force your child to do too much homework simply because more books are available. Reading another text and just reading each homework problem of an extra text may be sufficient to broaden mathematical studies without needing to do twice the homework load. When excessive pushing of mathematics leads to the exclusion of other activities, the attempt will sometimes backfire, and your child could decide that she does not want to continue pursuing her interest in math.

> As a college student, I always used both the required text and one or two others. I was interested to see how other authors would use the mathematics to investigate ideas, and I found the mathematics more comprehensible as I viewed it from multiple vantage points.
> —University Mathematics Faculty Member

Modifying the Depth of Mathematics

Conceptual Understanding Versus Procedural Knowledge

Broader mathematical fields can be likened to real-world application of mathematics. Deeper mathematics can best be described as looking at *why* mathematics happens as it does and *what* certain mathematical concepts really mean. Typically, students are asked to *use* mathematics and *do* mathematics, but rarely are they asked why a mathematical technique works or what a mathematical definition means. Answering these types of questions brings depth to math.

Mathematics teachers know that students can often solve equations, but be completely unable to justify why each step of the solution is valid. They are unable to associate a particular mathematical rule to the processes they follow. While they may be able to label the justifications for each step of a problem solved as an example in a text, they can rarely do so independently on their own solutions. This demonstrates that a much deeper understanding of what they so often perform mechanically exists, but they have not mastered this depth of understanding. Often, students can mimic techniques without fully understanding the depth of the mathematics included within the steps of the solution. Even though most students have seen the properties of the real numbers (also called the field axioms), they rarely fully associate the properties of the numbers with the processes they perform daily.

There exists a great realm of mathematics that is deeper and requires more understanding than the mathematics commonly seen by most students. Most often, students encounter bits and pieces of this extended realm through the classroom. Excellent mathematics teachers may carefully present measured amounts of deeper mathematical study to their classes, and textbooks occasionally allude to these deeper considerations.

> Students are often able to do a great deal of mathematics without fully and deeply understanding the fundamental concepts that support what they are doing. Students inevitably hit roadblocks because they lack the understanding of why they can do such and such and what effect one technique has on others. My highest goal is to build students' conceptual understanding —High School Mathematics Teacher

With appropriate prodding from you and your mathematically advanced student, teachers are often able to expand these investigations if your child is capable of learning more.

Distinguishing deeper mathematics from common mathematics has been summarized by a number of researchers as the difference between computational (or procedural) knowledge and conceptual understanding. Many students are able to mechanically perform mathematical manipulations and solve mathematical equations. Many are able to replicate what teachers demonstrate, and many are able to satisfy a teacher's goals by just *doing* mathematics. Most students, however, are only one well-choreographed question away from being lost, and demonstrating that their understanding of mathematics is grounded on procedures and calculations, and not upon deeper understanding of mathematical concepts underlying the procedural work.

Asking Why

As previously mentioned, asking why a mathematical procedure works often greatly deepens the mathematical investigation. Your advanced mathematics student often may be more curious about the hows and whys of the mathematics they are encountering. No end of possible investigations arise by simply asking why mathematical concepts and procedures work. To some extent, it is often unfortunate how quickly why questions go beyond the comprehensibility of traditional students. Mathematicians go to great lengths in sophisticated writings to examine the whys of mathematics, but these discussions usually can be understood only by advanced students. Some publishers of mathematical texts specialize in this genre, but most K–12 students must access elevated discussions of mathematical topics by reading college-level textbooks on similar topics. Some graduate-level texts may also be appropriate, depending on the topic.

Many topics in the K–12 curricula are reinvestigated in far greater depth in undergraduate and graduate mathematics courses. Ideas in algebra, probability, statistics, functions, number systems, and countless other topics, which are only shallowly addressed in K–12 classes, are expanded upon throughout entire college courses. As high school algebra students casually discuss the continuity of functions, university calculus and analysis students work their way to fuller understanding. In many cases, providing advanced high school students with college textbooks provides an experience that deepens the mathematics they are studying.

It would be convenient if their teachers knew the answers when K–12 students asked why certain mathematical procedures worked in such a manner. Unfortunately, they often do not. This is not intended to criticize the work and knowledge of K–12 teachers, because in many cases, the teachers knew the correct answers to why questions in years past. But, years and even decades, of teaching a specific and limited content may dull teachers' understanding and remembrance of the why questions.

> I once saw a teacher challenge his more advanced students by providing them with a list of definitions and theorems, some of which were correct and some were incorrect. Students had to determine which statements were correct and which were not, explain the error, and provide an example as to why the statement was incorrect.
> —University Mathematics Faculty Member

Digging Through Definitions

Elementary and secondary mathematics textbooks are filled with mathematical definitions and theorems. Often, however, these definitions and theorems are applied with less than adequate understanding. Students are provided definitions and rarely asked satisfactorily probing questions to ensure that they fully understand the meaning of the definition. Ask the average high school student to explain the meaning of most definitions and they will probably be lost. However, if an advanced student is challenged to be able to explain these concepts, he will probably relish the opportunity to dig deeper until first he can understand them, and then he can explain them.

Changing Mathematics

Another technique to significantly deepen mathematical investigations for advanced students is to ask them what would change if one simple alteration to a definition or theorem were allowed. These seemingly benign questions can often lead to unimaginable investigations.

> I read a book about mathematics that was written in the form of a play. The play's characters examined the mathematics that would be developed if it had been originally based on inequality (< or >) rather than equality (=). My students enjoyed working with the play to see the profound changes that would arise from a simple change in the original premise.
> —High School Mathematics Teacher

Problem Posing

One technique that greatly enhances mathematical investigation is to ask students to create their own mathematical questions. This practice is quite unusual, as students more often are asked to answer problems than to create them. However, few practices more clearly demonstrate a student's understanding of the mathematics. The problems students create demonstrate whether they clearly understand the mathematics, the constraints of the mathematics, and the extension of the mathematics. Often students create overly simplistic problems, and at other times they create problems that are too difficult for them to solve. This latter scenario opens another avenue of investigation for further mathematical knowledge. An example of this would be: *Explain the difference between empirical and theoretical probability. Then develop two problems, one that necessitates the use of empirical probability and one that necessitates the use of theoretical probability.*

Differentiating Mathematical Subjects From Mathematical Depth
More advanced mathematics differs from looking more deeply into mathematics. For nearly every topic discussed in K–12 math classes, students only scratch the surface of the depth of the topic. Within the cognitive ranges of these students, mathematics can be investigated more deeply. Mathematics is a vast enterprise, and only limited investigations are possible at each grade level. Time constraints force concentration on some topics and concepts and limit others. Many mathematical concepts can be investigated from numerous perspectives. Therefore, to deepen students' mathematical study does not necessarily mean to direct them toward study of more advanced mathematical subjects.

Any mathematical concept is sufficiently rich for unending study by K–12 students. There is no need, for instance, to study calculus in order to more deeply investigate algebra. Algebra, in and of itself, abounds with rich, deep, and meaningful notions that could take years to master. Indeed, extensions are always possible in algebra, making its study inexhaustible.

The following miniplay provides an introduction to some deeper understanding of algebra and number systems. In this example, students are gaining deeper understanding without necessarily delving into different mathematical subjects.

Jen and Mike are trying to solve an equation.

Mike: The problem says to attempt to solve the equation in the natural number system and discuss your findings. $3x + 5 = 10$.

Jen: That's an easy equation. It should be easy.

Mike: Well, let's see. First, I want to subtract 5 from both sides in order to get the term with the x by itself.

Jen: But, I don't think that we are allowed to subtract in the natural number system, because subtraction is not closed.

Mike: So instead I'll add the opposite of five to both sides.

Jen: But, that doesn't work either. Negative numbers do not exist in the natural numbers. The system does not have additive inverses.

Mike: Maybe that is what we were supposed to see, that this equation needs to be considered in a higher number system to be solved. Subtraction is closed in the integers and it has additive inverses. Maybe we can finish this problem in the integers.

Jen: OK, so we add the opposite of 5 to both sides and get $3x = 5$. Now let's divide each side by 3.

Mike: But, division is not closed in the integers. Nor do we have multiplicative inverses. So I suppose we have to now go to the rational numbers. Or, maybe we should just skip to the reals.

Jen: No, let's not skip too far ahead. Let's try the rational numbers and see what we get. If we multiply both sides by ⅓, then we get $x = ⅗$. That's our solution.

Mike: So, even though the problem looked simple, we couldn't solve it in the natural numbers, whole numbers, or even the integers.

Jen: What type of equation would we need in order to have to solve it in the reals?

Mike: I'm not sure, but I think that as long as the equation has only addition, subtraction, multiplication, and division, it can be solved in the rational numbers, because all these operations are closed in the rational number system.

Jen: But, what other operations are there?

Mike: Exponents and roots.

Jen: But, exponents are just repeated multiplication.

Mike: I know. But, solving exponents and roots don't always work.

Jen: What do you mean? You can always take a root of a number. But, it's not always a rational number. Sometimes it's irrational or imaginary.

Mike: You're right. But, irrational numbers are real numbers. So roots are OK as long as we are taking even roots of numbers that are not negative. We can take odd roots of any numbers.

This miniplay demonstrates an integration of a number of mathematical concepts:
- linear equations;
- solutions to equations;
- properties of the real numbers (closure, equality, zero, commutative, associative, distributive, identity, and inverse properties); and
- number systems (natural, whole, integers, rational, irrational, real, and complex numbers).

Although these number systems are utilized beginning in the earliest grades and the properties are developed as a student matures in mathematical understanding, there are many years of study needed in order to fully understand these more elementary concepts. This demonstrates how mathematical investigations can be deepened without looking to different subjects altogether.

Enriching Mathematical Investigations With the NCTM Principles and Standards

The National Council of Teachers of Mathematics (NCTM) has developed the *Principles and Standards* (2000), which guides teachers and curriculum decision makers to a unified philosophy of education. This book supports the need for children who are advanced in mathematics to receive appropriately challenging mathematics instruction. NCTM's *Principles and Standards* promotes the following fundamental principles: equity, curriculum, teaching, learning, assessment, and technology. These are discussed in more detail in Table 7.

NCTM's principles can be used to extend and deepen mathematical investigations. Equity, curriculum, teaching, learning, assessment, and technology all work in harmony to argue that the proper role of mathematics in K–12 education is to empower each student to reach his or her full academic potential and become productive citizens. Therefore, these principles will support your claims regarding the individual needs of your mathematically advanced child. The unique needs of each child necessitate unique applications of curriculum.

NCTM's principles should all work in tandem to meet the needs of all children and every child individually. You should not hesitate to use NCTM's book and recommendations to suggest to schools and teachers that your child needs curricular accommodation. NCTM's process standards (problem solving, reasoning and proof, communication, connections, and representation) demonstrate pathways to more advanced mathematical investigations. Unfortunately, many teachers have not recognized how these process standards can be utilized to direct advanced students toward deeper mathematical investigations. The following

Table 7
NCTM's Principles and Standards

Principles:

The six principles for school mathematics demonstrate NCTM's philosophical beliefs of important themes in student learning:

- *Equity*: All students deserve excellent education and the support they need to succeed.
- *Curriculum*: The curriculum that students receive should be coherent within each grade and across all grades and must concentrate on important mathematics.
- *Teaching*: Quality teaching requires deep understanding of student needs and learning and must challenge students to excel and support their success.
- *Learning*: Students learn as they experience mathematics and integrate new knowledge with the knowledge they previously possessed.
- *Assessment*: Assessment should be continual and should both evaluate student knowledge and inform the teacher in which direction to head for the student to learn most effectively.
- *Technology:* Mathematical learning can be significantly enhanced by the appropriate use of technology.

Standards:

The Content Standards explicitly describe the content that students should learn. These include:

- number and operations,
- algebra,
- geometry,
- measurement, and
- data analysis and probability.

The Process Standards illuminate how students learn the necessary content knowledge. These include:

- problem solving,
- reasoning and proof,
- communication,
- connections, and
- representation.

Note. Compiled from *Principles and Standards of School Mathematics*, by National Council of Teachers of Mathematics, 2000.

sections demonstrate application of each of the process standards for students to interact more with mathematics.

NCTM's Process Standards

Problem Solving

Within *Principles and Standards*, problem solving takes a central role. It is argued that students learn better when they are actively engaged in the problem-solving process. The historic method of teachers lecturing to students has been, to some degree or another, replaced by problem-based instruction. In other words, through the process of attempting to solve a problem, students become actively involved in learning mathematics. They then learn both the included mathematics and skills to assist them in solving additional problems in the future.

We can all remember how certain tasks have captivated us in the past. We can all remember countless hours spent on a project, puzzle, hobby, book, or even school assignment in which we were interested. In these moments, we became so involved with the project that learning became a secondary byproduct. Indeed, this scenario falls in line with NCTM's recommendations. NCTM recommends that the problems students encounter should be important, significant, interesting, engaging, challenging, worthwhile, and connected to the real-world experiences and interests of students. Notably, in order for problems to meet all of these expectations, they must originate from the innate interests of the problem solver.

Care must be taken to differentiate difficult problems from rich and meaningful problems. All too frequently, teachers who are attempting to enrich a student's mathematical experience by introducing problem-solving curricula simply select problems that are more difficult. Often these more advanced problems are well beyond the student's ability. It is much better to find problems that are on, or slightly above, the student's ability level that require unconventional thinking.

What does this focus on problem solving do to typical classroom assignments and homework? The old handouts with dozens of mind-numbing exercises are gone. There is now an important distinction between exercises and problems. Exercises can be likened to practice, whereas problems can be likened to active investigations. Thus, it is entirely possible that one well-choreographed problem addresses a greater number of concepts, modalities of thinking, and skill sets than dozens of rote, repetitious exercises.

Clearly, the selection of appropriate problems is the teacher's greatest challenge. Little generic advice can be given to teachers regarding this charge, because the individuality of each student is precisely what determines the appropriateness of each problem and whether that problem is sufficiently interesting to the student to keep his or her attention through the problem-solving process. Nevertheless, you should communicate with schools and know how your child's teachers anticipate extending the mathematical experiences of advanced mathematics through problem solving.

Characteristics of a Meaningful Problem

Most mathematics educators today would agree with this simple statement: *Students learn mathematics more efficiently when they encounter and are involved in solving meaningful problems.* In order to fully understand this statement, it is necessary to come to some agreement regarding a couple of the terms embedded in the statement.

Learning mathematics does not simply mean mastering a skill. It means learning to reason mathematically and understand mathematics as a tool for problem solving. It also means using mathematics, as well as doing mathematics. Thus, learning mathematics includes understanding why something works and not merely the steps needed to perform a certain operation. Learning mathematics in this way is best accomplished through students actively participating in problem-solving experiences. Therefore, a teacher, tutor, or parent's selection of mathematical experiences and problems for a student needs to be deeply considered. Problem selection for a student should never be done haphazardly. Problem selection should be recognized as an integral part of mathematical learning, and growth in problem-solving ability should be valued very highly alongside the accompanying skills.

It is necessary to understand the notion of *problem* versus *exercise*. A problem is a scenario in which, upon initiation, neither the result nor a method for solution is known. An exercise is a scenario in which the result is unknown but a method for solution is known. Interestingly, what may be an exercise for one student may be a problem for another. Furthermore, when students do not know a method to solve a scenario, even though they should, it is a problem until they learn a method for solution; then it becomes an exercise. Within any group of supposed exercises (e.g., at the end of sections and chapters in texts), as concepts are further investigated, selected examples may indeed be problems to some students. This is often the case when examples look alike and yet methods for solutions change due to alterations among the examples. Therefore, factoring $90x^2 + 27x + 40$ may be an exercise to a precalculus student, but a problem to an Algebra I or II student who lacks the necessary foundation.

Problem selection, however, also includes a concern for *meaningful problems*. Meaningful problems can often be confused with overly difficult problems. While meaningful problems are often challenging, they are more centered on the interests of the learner than the actual content of the mathematics. The following list describes some of the characteristics of meaningful mathematics problems. Meaningful problems are:

- *Connected.* Students live and participate in the real world and they have interests in the real world. Mathematics is not separated from the real world, it is intricately woven into it. Meaningful mathematics continually demonstrates to students how mathematics affects their real lives. Additionally, mathematics is connected internally; many mathematical concepts are connected to others. Meaningful mathematics problems reveal that problems can be solved in many ways using ideas from a variety of connected mathematical concepts.

- *Important.* Meaningful mathematics problems look at mathematical topics that are mathematically important and central to the learning of the students. Teachers, parents, and tutors must understand the big picture of mathematics and how ideas interconnect and build upon each other. Focusing on important mathematics can be very economical and can better meet the needs of advanced students, as they can often learn less important mathematics independently.

- *Significant.* Students may not always understand the mathematical importance of a problem. Nevertheless, they must find that the problem is significant to them. Some questions that students independently raise will be significant to them, but may lack significant mathematical importance. Teachers must understand their students and what the students will find significant. Students are not apt to want to work on mathematics that they find insignificant. Occasionally, when students do not perceive the importance of a mathematical idea and why a concept should be significant to the students, teachers will need to demonstrate why certain concepts should be mathematically significant to them.

- *Interesting.* Problems should be interesting to students. This may mean contextualizing problems in the world of the student or demonstrating how a problem may affect them. However, not every problem needs to be taken directly out of the life of the student in order to be interesting. Many students find certain problems interesting because of the mathematics included in the investigation or how uniquely the problem is posed. The world is full of mathematics and mathematical problems; teaching experience introduces educators to innumerable problems that are interesting to individuals and classes of students. It is important for teachers to ground their mathematics instructions, as much as possible, in interesting mathematics posed in interesting ways.

- *Engaging.* Many problems can be important, significant, and interesting, but may not be significant enough to captivate a student's focus and engage him in the problem-solving process. Engaging problems draw the student into the investigation; she is almost compelled to work at the problem until she comes to some resolution.

- *Challenging.* Some problems are simply too easy to be meaningful. Learning occurs both by solving a problem and through the problem-solving process itself. Students do not become adequately interested and engaged in problems that they immediately perceive as easily solved.

Being an advanced student? It was fun for a while, being the quickest can be cool. But, I got bored. I hated being the only one raising my hand. I was young and my peers' resentment still battered me. The worst was when you started pushing the teachers' boundaries; it got to the point where they didn't want you asking questions anymore. —University Student

- *Worthwhile.* When energy is expended solving a problem, students must have some assurance that the process and the results are worthwhile in respect to what will be learned. After years of solving problems in academic scenarios, students intuitively perform a cost-benefit analysis of all they do. They are unwilling to fully engage in tasks in which they lack confidence that the learning and experiences gained will be worth the efforts involved in the problem-solving process.

Reasoning and Proof

Students know that a number cannot be divided by zero, and that division by zero is undefined. Countless other mathematical concepts confront students on a daily basis. Unfortunately, in many cases, students are asked to accept the mathematical statement with little or no justification. NCTM's focus on reasoning and proof, however, does not imply that students should be able to prove all the mathematics they encounter. Rather, it means that some concepts should be proven and others should be accompanied by deeper understanding, but few should be accepted blindly and without understanding.

Reasoning is central to deepening mathematical understanding. Mathematics educators can create somewhat open-ended problems in order to lead students toward greater reasoning. Rather than asking a student to solve a particular problem, a student may be asked how a certain concept relates to another. He or she may be asked to explain why some mathematical concept produces the results it does, or if it would produce similar results if one or more of the components in the concept changed.

One powerful method for enhancing reasoning and proof is to ask students how a concept in one area of mathematics relates to another seemingly unconnected area of mathematics. For example, how does the intersection of two sets relate to the conjunction in logic? Or, how does the law of large numbers connect probability theory to statistics?

The ability to reason through various levels of mathematical understanding opens the door to increasingly advanced study. More topics and concepts are attainable by those students who are able to reason through more elementary concepts. However, skillfully guiding students toward reasoning in mathematics is not commonly within the ability of beginning teachers. Care must be taken to avoid asking students to reason far beyond what they are prepared to do, as this can frustrate students. A rare number of students are able to take any mathematical enterprise as a bona fide challenge; most students will find anything that is overly challenging to be frustrating. Therefore, you should meet with your child's teachers and ask how they will challenge him to reason more deeply, and how this will lead to further mathematical investigation.

Reasoning and proof are extremely contingent upon your child's cognitive and academic abilities. Clearly, proving mathematical theorems is not a typical assignment for most elementary or middle school students. Conversely, reasoning why the sum of two numbers takes the sign of the number with the greatest absolute value may be too elementary for senior high students. Thus, no generic reasoning exercise fits all students and, in order to maximize learning, the development of reasoning skills must be individualized for each student.

As mentioned previously regarding problem solving, more difficult mathematical problems or topics do not necessarily equate to deeper mathematical reasoning. In addition, carefully crafted problems consistent with the ability of the student do not need to include mathematical topics other than what the student is already considering. Simply asking your child to verify some of the mathematics she is already using can provide an enormous amount of fodder for mathematical reasoning and proof.

Communication

NCTM advocates that communication be a central component of student learning, as students must learn to communicate their mathematical understanding. Although NCTM recommends that students be able to communicate their mathematical understanding in many forms—written, orally, and diagrammatically—it should be understood that communication leads to learning and not simply presentation. Students learn as they share ideas and communicate to each other. Thus, communication is both the process and the result of learning.

Mathematicians know the satisfaction that is derived by writing mathematically. Mathematics has its own language and style of writing. While it is concise, often even overly terse, it also allows creativity. Writing mathematically often incorporates decisions about representational style and technique, and different writers can explain and develop mathematical ideas in very different ways. Some may use diagrams, some may use examples, and some may use more concise symbolization. Sometimes, the writer even needs to invent mathematical symbols and verbiage in order to communicate ideas. Advanced mathematics students should be encouraged to communicate mathematically, and they should be led to communicate mathematical ideas and be mentored into precise reasoning and language.

> Our professor had us read a lot of mathematics books and papers. Then we had to either explain them orally or write extensive explanations. We learned so much and became so much more comfortable with the math that I cannot imagine trying to learn another mathematics subject without reading and writing a lot. It was worth the pain.
> —University Student

Your child should learn to express his mathematical understanding through both verbal and written forms. Unfortunately, however, this learning and teaching tool is sometimes misunderstood by mathematics teachers. Teachers often ask students to write reports of the life, times, and discoveries of historic mathematicians or the historic development of a certain field of mathematics, and while these exercises are valuable, they miss the mark of NCTM's recommendation. Examples of more valuable assignments for older students might be:

- Explain the trichotomy property and describe at least three applications of it.
- Explain why division by zero is undefined.
- Explain what is meant by an equivalence relation and give examples of such in various fields of mathematics.
- For a given system of equations, discuss everything going on at a selected point. Use every field of mathematics you have studied.

These communication-dense assignments provide students with opportunities to communicate what they know, realize gaps in their understanding, and learn materials necessary to fill those gaps. In doing so, your child will be able to learn mathematics beyond the concepts immediately at hand.

Mathematical Connections

NCTM recommends that students investigate mathematics by considering two types of connections. First, mathematical ideas should be investigated as they cross mathematical fields and topics. For instance, many concepts among set theory and logic connect the two fields of study (i.e., intersection of sets and conjunction of statements, union of sets and disjunction of statements, subsets and conditional statements, set equality and logically equivalent statements). These internal connections inside mathematics provide a framework through which advanced mathematics students can extend their learning. So extensive are these internal connections that no one could possibly catalog them all. This extensiveness creates a dynamic dimension by which mathematically advanced students can broaden their mathematical knowledge. Rather than haphazardly skipping from one mathematical topic to another, a central theme may be used through which to investigate connected mathematical ideas.

Connections also can be made between mathematics and other interests. Art, music, mechanics, electronics, computer networking, architecture, poetry, bikes, exercise, and countless other interests can all be investigated from a mathematical perspective. Through these external connections between math and other concerns, students can investigate math as it relates to their own interests. For parents and teachers to verify the plethora of topics that can be investigated mathematically, a simple Google search connecting a field of interest and the word *mathematics* can produce more results than most would believe possible.

External connections are usually characterized as connections between mathematical concepts and real-world phenomena. Examples of these connections continue to be published in textbooks, journals, and other books. This is a very popular genre of mathematical investigation and publication today. Students can generally find publications of connections between mathematics and their

> My favorite math teacher made us look at logic, set theory, number theory, probability, and graph theory all together to better understand how they were connected. We had to use the mathematics in the course to investigate one of our hobbies or interests outside of mathematics. We really learned a lot of math, but we also learned how valuable it was. —University Student

other favorite topics. Math will seem to become more animated to your child as he applies his studies to his favorite hobby.

Before assigning students to mathematically investigate real-world phenomena, teachers must be very cautious. Very often, the mathematics involved in real-world phenomena quickly becomes very advanced and beyond the scope of most students. Judiciously selecting which investigations to allow students to follow becomes a major concern for teachers. However, students' interests and enthusiasm in certain pursuits often mitigate the difficulty involved in the investigation. When students are mesmerized in the investigation of an issue of interest, they have the ability to persevere through difficult studies. They press on through one concept after another until they master that in which they are interested. A delicate balance, then, exists: Students will work harder to learn the mathematics regarding something in which they are interested, but they may quickly become daunted if the mathematical investigations are too abruptly complex beyond the students' abilities.

Representations

Lastly, in the process standards, NCTM recommends that students become aware of, and learn to use, multiple representations of mathematical ideas. These include verbal, tabular (numeric), symbolic (algebraic), and graphical representations. As mathematical ideas can be represented in a number of commonly recognized ways, multiple representations can be used to deepen mathematical discussions (see Figure 2).

Symbolic representations may be the most commonly recognized representation of algebra. It includes numbers, variables, and equations. Graphical representations are also common; these often include graphs, plots, and charts. Tabular (or numeric) representations are somewhat less common as solutions to problems.

Unfortunately, tables of numeric data are often considered to be the beginning of the problem rather than a viable form of solution. Today's emphasis on multiple representations has led to the understanding that tables can be valid answers. The verbal representation includes written and oral presentations of mathematical concepts. When one or more of these representations leads to another, we denote this as multiple representations.

The use of multiple representations can significantly deepen the mathematics being investigated by posing mathematical questions in unconventional form. Mathematical questions, which may typically originate in symbolic form (such as the problem: "Graph the function $y = 3x^2 + 4x + 3$"), may also be reversed (as in a prompt to determine the equation that would produce a given graph). Moreover, investigating problems that necessitate the use of simultaneous representations can deepen mathematical investigations. Examples of the use of multiple representations are numerous and easily individualized for different students, making it impossible to generalize one or two examples appropriate for all learners.

Using multiple representations is NCTM's newest process standard. While fewer teachers will be aware of how to use multiple representations as an instructional technique and appreciate the value of multiple representations as a tool for learning, most mathematics teachers will have experienced many hours of professional development and workshops demonstrating the use of multiple representations in the classroom.

The use of multiple representations in mathematics learning can be profound. Multiple representations allow students to investigate mathematics in respect to their own learning styles and preferences. Interestingly, using multiple representations to enhance mathematical experiences may be significantly easier for teachers, and require the least additional training. In many cases,

The following demonstrates the meaning and application of multiple representations:

Verbal: A person earns $1 on the first day, $2 on the second day, $4 on the third day, $8 on the fourth day, and so forth. How much money would they have at the end of 2 weeks?

Numeric (tabular):

Day	Earnings
1	1
2	2
3	4
4	8
5	16

Symbolic: *EarningsPerDay* or 2^{Day-1} or $y = 2^{x-1}$

Graphical:

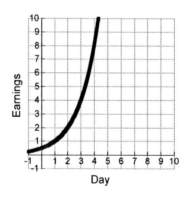

Figure 2. Multiple Mathematical Representations

teachers will be doing little more than tightly integrating techniques they have previously left disconnected.

Using the Process Standards

Altogether, NCTM's process standards form rich pathways to learning and deepening mathematical understanding. So, how can you use these process standards to address the needs of your mathematically advanced child in school? First, it should be understood that some teachers are not completely familiar with NCTM's recommendations and the applications of the recommendations in the classroom. Thus, as you speak with K–12 educators, you can and should inquire how these process standards will be used in your child's instruction and advancement.

Second, when teachers are aware of these process standards they will come to realize that providing appropriate instruction and curriculum to advanced mathematics students need not mean that new courses must be developed. Rather, teachers can simply use the processes by which students naturally learn to enhance their curriculum and the learning experience.

Third, you will be empowered if you can use documents that the educational community values in your negotiation with schools and teachers. If you have done your homework in support of your child, this will undoubtedly impress teachers and administrators. Armed with NCTM's (2000) *Principles and Standards for School Mathematics*, you will be recognized as a parent who possesses scholarly justification for his or her concerns and requests.

Alternatives to Traditional Schooling

You may find that you need to investigate other educational opportunities for your child if your local school is unable or unwilling to provide the educational experience that your child needs. Charter schools, distance education, and homeschooling are viable alternatives to traditional schooling that can be valuable either as a supplement to the regular school experience or as a long-term substitute for regular schooling.

Charter Schools

Largely because of the problems in public and some private schools, many areas have been experimenting with charter schools of one kind or another. There are charter schools for practically any type of interest or need, whether it is a learning disability, a social or emotional problem, an interest in a particular subject or skill area, or a performance-based ability. There are even charter schools developed just for advanced children. If you are disappointed in the education your child is being offered in school, it might be wise to research the charter schools in your area.

I was so tired of wasting my time every day that I was just going to quit school after 11th grade and get my GED. When my mom found a charter school that would let me do online courses and go to college at the same time, I did that and graduated from high school with college credits, too.
—Charter School Graduate

Distance Education

Distance education has been available for generations in the form of correspondence schools. Elementary and high school students who were unable to attend their local school regularly due to illness or extensive travel were able to continue their studies and graduate from high school through these correspondence schools. The advent of the computer and Internet has radically changed the landscape for distance education, and parents and students are becoming aware of the flexibility it can offer. Students may now use online courses to accelerate and progress at their own pace in one course or their entire school experience.

Schools are also finding they can offer their students more appropriate content and pace through the use of Internet-based courses. In addition, many schools are forming partnerships with other districts to offer coursework via teleconferencing so that a teacher can interact in real time with a group of advanced students who are not physically in the same room. This method of delivery is helpful when a district has too few students in need of advanced learning to create a particular course.

Homeschooling

Homeschooling is an option that you may want to consider if you find that your school either can't or won't meet your child's educational needs. Originally chosen by parents for religious or health-related reasons, homeschooling has become much more popular recently. This is in part because of the availability of online courses students can take via the Internet. When students participate in an online course, the parent no longer bears the responsibility of being the primary teacher for that subject.

Homeschooling has also benefited from the increase in community co-ops or networks, where families get together and each parent chooses a subject area to teach to the group of children. In this way, each parent is able to teach a subject area in which they excel, and they can spend time developing their lessons. The

> Homeschooling was supposed to be a hoot. I was looking forward to doing all of my schoolwork in 2 or 3 hours, but Mom thought I should keep the same hours at home as I did at school, and get much more done because I could work at my own speed. This caused friction. —Homeschooled Student

children benefit from the social interaction, as well as the increase in the quality of lessons they experience.

Schools are now more welcoming to homeschoolers, too. Some schools allow the homeschooled children to participate in sports and other extracurricular activities. In some areas, districts have lost so many students to homeschooling that they have found it necessary to make fundamental changes in their philosophies and operations in order to woo the homeschoolers back into the schools so that they can again receive state reimbursement for the increased enrollment.

I was homeschooled all the way through high school, and I think homeschooling offers some significant advantages for gifted students. The curriculum is entirely self-paced; one never needs to spend any more or less time on a given concept than it takes to understand it. A prolearning environment is much easier to foster in the home.
—University Student

Summary of Key Points

- You should display a positive attitude and strive to develop and maintain a partnership with school personnel.
- Because children who are advanced in mathematics are individuals, the program that is best for a particular child is an individualized one.
- You will need to work with school personnel and use the results of the comprehensive evaluation to determine the level and type of curricular modification your child needs.
- There are many ways to modify the curriculum in mathematics.
- You can use the recommendations presented in the NCTM *Principles and Standards* book to assist the school in designing an appropriate program for your child.

- There are valuable alternatives to traditional schooling such as charter schools, online and distance education, and homeschooling.

Questions to Ask Your Child:

- Do you wish to work in the school system or out of the school system to enhance your mathematics?
- Do you wish to take more advanced classes or go into more depth in your mathematical studies?
- Do you feel that your school can give you the assistance you need?
- What has the school been doing for you already?
- Would you like to skip grades in mathematics?
- Would you like to be grouped with other advanced students?
- Would you prefer an alternative to public schooling, like a charter school, some distance education, or homeschooling?

Questions to Ask the School:

- What type of training do you provide for your teachers of advanced students?
- What programs do you have in place in your school for advanced mathematics students?
- What collaborative educational efforts do you have in place with universities and colleges for advanced students?
- How does the school address concerns such as: more of the same, piled higher; using students as teachers or tutors; every child gets the same; and topical redundancy in a subject area?

Questions to Ask Your Child's Mathematics Teacher:

- Do you feel qualified and capable to take my child to higher levels in mathematics?
- How would you enhance the pace, breadth, and depth of instruction for mathematically advanced students?

Chapter 3

Supporting the Mathematically Advanced Child in the Home

I n the previous chapter, recommendations were provided regarding how you could obtain appropriate support from the school system for your mathematically advanced child. Unfortunately, some parents may find working with the school system too difficult and less than fulfilling. Other parents may prefer to homeschool their child. In either case, you may decide to find educational enhancement opportunities for your child outside of the regular school system. In this chapter, we will discuss ways to provide support for your child through avenues that are not directly offered by his or her school.

In this chapter, you will gain information regarding:

• community resources and mentors,

- encouraging children to discover mathematics on their own, and
- technological tools to enrich math learning.

A number of subtopics are covered within each of these categories. These will guide you to the many ways in which mathematically advanced students can be supported through resources from the home. Admittedly, these resources often have costs associated with them. Herein, again, they differ from school-based resources, which are most often free to parents and children. In this chapter, materials and opportunities are discussed along with the associated costs of many resources.

The Math-Positive Home

The home can play an important role in the mathematical development of any child. Your home can be made into a math-positive environment—one that encourages mathematics use and investigation. The following brief list provides some suggestions for making your home math positive.

- You should continually speak positively about mathematics, mathematical experiences, and careers that require mathematical skills. It is especially important to encourage your child to look at mathematical pursuits and math-based careers. Many children are initially interested in scientific pursuits, but are discouraged from them by their parents and pressures from their friends who do not share mathematical and scientific interests.
- Be sure to involve your child in decision making, planning, and activities that necessitate mathematical skills and reasoning. For instance, properly selecting an appropriate cell

phone plan for the family necessitates a great deal of analysis of family needs and correlation with options provided through various plans.

- You should encourage your child to watch age-appropriate TV programming that positively portrays mathematical and scientific pursuits. Programs that portray forensic scientists are currently very popular. Many programs on engineering marvels can also be valuable.

- Your home should have abundant reading resources regarding mathematics and science. Books at every age level should be provided that discuss the lives, discoveries, and inventions of famous mathematicians and scientists.

- If your family has a computer and Internet access, encyclopedia software and Web sites should be provided to your child to feed her curiosity when she wishes to investigate an issue.

- Family conversations should be turned to mathematics often. When your child asks a question about any interest, you may wish to reformulate the question into one framed in mathematics. For instance, if your child is interested in cars, you may ask him to compare car prices to the cost of car ownership (taxes, insurance, gas mileage, maintenance costs, expected longevity, etc.).

- Many types of educational materials exist for younger mathematics students. Your young child can participate in hands-on activities and play with brightly colored solid shapes, leading to mathematical understanding. Geometric shapes can be purchased at education supply stores or on the Internet.

- Your home should be well-equipped with scales, balances, rulers, levels, plumb bobs, string, elastics, weights, measuring cups and spoons, magnifying glasses, microscopes, and telescopes. The ready availability of measuring devices allows for interesting questions to be immediately investigated.

- Mathematical puzzle books should be in your home, so that your child can learn that he can use mathematics for fun activities. In addition, you can show your child how to use mathematics to develop strategies to play common board games. More advanced students may be asked whether kicking an extra point or going for two is a better strategical decision for a football team.

Creating a mathematically positive home environment not only promotes mathematics in the home, but also provides a sanctuary for children who are interested in mathematics and science, but are discouraged from mathematical pursuits by their friends and classmates in schools. Many children begin to avoid mathematics only after they are taught that they are expected to by people outside of the family.

> I recommend that parents of gifted children challenge them as much as possible. I had problem-solving books, games, and flash cards to challenge me at home. Until I received extra attention at school and was afforded the opportunity to stretch my knowledge, I did not have a lot of interest in school.
> —Student

School Readiness for Preschool Students

School readiness is important for all preschool children. Possessing certain understandings and skills in mathematics greatly increases your child's ability to learn mathematics. The following is a list of skills that you can help your child develop prior to entering school and through the earliest years of schooling.

- Remembering word number sequence (one, two, three . . .)
- Counting objects
- Sorting and categorizing objects
- Recognizing numerals

- Recognizing and extending patterns
- Adding (by counting objects)
- Subtracting (by removing objects)
- Measuring (with rulers or measuring cups)
- Multiplying (by repeated addition). Care must be taken to not force children too quickly into multiplication (memorizing flash cards) without simultaneously developing some understanding of the meaning of multiplication. Only unusually advanced children are able to understand and perform multiplication at early ages—some as early as 2 years old. Because this is not usually covered in school until second or third grade, it is not necessary to push preschoolers into this area unless they are prepared to do so. If they are ready, they should not be held back from considering this.
- Dividing (by set partition). Again, forcing division facts (flash cards) upon children who are not yet ready to understand the meaning of division is both unnecessary and potentially counterproductive, instilling confusion and frustration on the part of a child who is asked to recite what he or she does not understand.
- Knowing the alphabet and reading. Many students in school suffer mathematically because they have difficulty reading. Word problems and mathematical explanations and directions are very difficult for children who read below grade level. Any assistance that you provide to help your child to learn to read will also help with mathematical understandings.

Tutors and Mentors

One of the greatest strengths of academically advanced students may also serve as one of their greatest obstacles. Advanced students are often independent learners and therefore need additional academic assistance far less often than average students. They learn to navigate their way through their respective studies. When in further need of understanding an assignment, advanced students tend to seek only the support of those few other students in their academic clique. They rarely seek additional assistance from educational professionals or parents.

This practice of academic cloistering and avoiding assistance may limit academically advanced students from access to sources of rich enrichment. In nearly every community there exist numerous people with advanced mathematical skills. Teachers, college students, university professors, and professionals can be sources of enrichment for mathematically advanced K–12 students. However, because these students infrequently need assistance from other groups of people, they rarely seek them out for enrichment. Thus, you must make the necessary connections between your child and other resources.

Prior to deciding from where and whom to first ask for assistance for a mathematically advanced student, you and your child should decide what type of assistance you need and want. Most commonly, two types of assistance are sought, namely tutoring and mentoring. Each has its strengths and weaknesses.

Tutoring is most commonly an arrangement in which students are guided through various academic disciplines. Mathematical tutoring may include the study of many levels of traditional scholastic mathematics. This tutoring may extend or deepen your child's regular classroom curriculum or go one or many grade levels beyond your child's chronological grade curriculum. Nevertheless, tutoring usually addresses mathematical topics found in traditional elementary, middle, and secondary grades, and undergraduate and graduate classes. Usually, but not exclusively, tutoring utilizes a textbook or curriculum of some sort. With these commonalities understood, it is also necessary to understand that tutoring can take many dissimilar forms. Tutoring may be one-on-one or one-on-many. It may be in a classroom, office, or home, and may take place daily, weekly, or monthly. Tutoring may even be on an as-needed basis with students primarily working independently through a text.

Tutoring provides some worthwhile benefits. First, students can master traditional math. This can significantly assist them to proceed more efficiently and effectively through subjects that they would encounter in their pursuit of mathematics. Tutoring also can be paced to best meet the individual student's needs. And, since traditional curricula are usually employed, tutoring can be somewhat less labor intensive for the tutor. Lastly, the tutoring paradigm can strictly control a student's workload.

> I felt like the dumbest kid in the gifted group, especially in early elementary school. My parents were smart but never went to college and didn't usually discuss highbrow academic topics. The gifted classes were so far removed from my comfort zone at home that I developed a resentment toward intellectuals and still don't really care for them today.
> —Student

Weaknesses associated with tutoring are also worth noting. Because tutoring usually covers traditional topics, some tutors may be diehard traditionalists who value the mathematics more than the students. Some tutors may not consider the child's needs or interests; rather, they will see the coverage of mathematical topics as the goal. In this way, mathematics, and not necessarily the student's progress, may become the focus of tutoring sessions.

Mentoring can take many forms, but the most significant distinction from tutoring is in the content and focus of the study. In the mentoring relationship, the mentor brings the child alongside him or her and guides the student toward mastery of what the mentor knows. However, the mentor's knowledge may be multifaceted beyond academics, and some mentors are recognized as having excelled in various endeavors. For instance, a woman may have become a very successful businessperson, and she may wish to impart some of her business savvy to a young student. An engineer or architect may wish to motivate the next generation in the field. An old craftsman may wish to preserve skills that may soon be lost. For example, many older craftsmen who practiced their trade before the advent of computers possess a wealth of mathematical and scientific knowledge that is now embedded and deeply hidden within software packages used by modern craftsmen in the field; this knowledge can be shared with younger students so they gain an appreciation for the mathematical calculations being performed within the software. This preservation and dissemination of knowledge and skills leads to a unique relationship between the mentor and student. The collaboration between the two is built upon the foundation of mutual interest, because both are interested in the mentor's field of expertise.

In the realm of mentoring, the application of mathematics generally outweighs the study of theoretical mathematics. Accountants, lawyers, engineers, business people, doctors, pharmacists, contractors, advertising agents, seamstresses, and people engaged in many other occupations apply mathematics daily to solve problems specific to their field. This kind of mathematics can be used as the foundation for worthwhile mathematical investigations. Mentors can pose interesting real-world problems for students to solve using fairly intricate mathematical models and processes. Thus, mathematics can be learned contextually in a need-to-know scenario that gives it life and interest. Indoor, outdoor, in offices, or in factories, wherever employment occurs, mentoring can take place.

One primary value of mentoring over tutoring is that along with mathematics, the student can learn a valuable trade and

- Will the mentor guide her through real-world problems that she faces daily?

These issues should be decided upon before you seek additional resources for your mathematically advanced child. In addition, you should always remember that no solution should be considered permanent. The needs of mathematically advanced students will change with time, so as your child's needs change, the solutions may also change. You can certainly find different tutors and mentors; you and your child are never trapped in one situation. More information on tutoring and mentoring can be found in Table 8.

Tutoring

You should first have an idea of the costs associated with tutoring, and often the level of commitment that you want for your child to receive will determine the expense. Local teachers, professors, college students, and others may be willing to tutor the student free of charge, but you should never assume that this will be the case. Although this may be a delicate issue to navigate for most parents and even most professional educators, it must be done carefully; no one, on either end of the transaction, wishes to later feel that the other had taken advantage of them. It is sometimes helpful to develop a contract that details the responsibilities of you, your child, and the tutor. A contract should include the number of contact hours between the tutor and your child, the number and amount of assignments between sessions, the content that will be covered by the tutor, the costs and frequency of pay, and the role that you are expected to play.

> The best thing parents can do for children who are mathematically inclined is give them opportunity after opportunity to further their understanding. Mathematically gifted students, if not allowed to reach their full potential, will become mathematically deprived.
> —Student

apply this to future employment opportunities. Secondly, the mathematics may seem more alive and applicable to life today. However, mentoring also has some significant drawbacks. For example, while mentors are well-versed in the mathematics they use, they often cannot wander very far outside of their domain. This leaves many connections to other fields of mathematics virtually untouched. In addition, the mathematics applied in some professions may be somewhat limited.

> My advice for parents of mathematically talented children: Don't push too hard or they will hate it! Always encourage but don't nag. Give them chances to grow, and help arrange transportation if they want to be involved in mathematical activities. Allow or help them look for programs for gifted/talented kids. —Student

It is important for you to realize that the distinctions between tutoring and mentoring are not always completely cut and dried. Many expert tutors can guide students through the fascinating world of applied mathematics and mentors may use a very textbook approach to the mentoring. In addition to reaching an agreement with your child regarding the type of assistance wanted, you should discuss and agree upon the time commitment and workload expectation for your child. If too much is required, your child may soon come to resent the additional work. If too little is required, she may fail to appreciate the efforts of both you and the support system. The following, and many more, questions should be answered prior to deciding on what type of mathematical enrichment your child should receive:

- How often will she meet with the tutor/mentor?
- Will the tutor direct instructional sessions, or will your child be guided as she investigates a topic of interest?
- Will the topics investigated be similar to, extensions of, or very different from that covered in her regular classroom?

Table 8
Tutoring Versus Mentoring

Similarities:
- Both tutoring and mentoring are performed by a person with greater mathematical knowledge (particularly in a certain field) than the student.
- Both have a goal of developing greater mathematical understanding in a student.
- Both are usually one-on-one.
- Both are usually performed on a fixed schedule.

Differences:
- Tutoring usually costs money, whereas mentoring is generally free.
- Mentoring is usually performed by someone who works in a field related to mathematics; for instance, mentors may be engineers, bankers, scientists, and the like. Mentors can be anyone who uses mathematics in his or her career.
- Tutors are generally more advanced students or educators. Teachers and professors can be mentors of promising mathematics students.
- Tutoring usually concentrates on mathematical topics directly associated with the mathematics being investigated in the school. Mentoring generally considers the mathematics associated with the mentor's occupation.
- Tutoring centers on mathematical studies. Mentoring centers on the interests of the students, and works to develop connections between scholastic mathematics and workplace mathematics.
- Tutoring involves little personal commitment on the part of the tutor. It is primarily a business arrangement. Mentoring is a more significant personal investment on the part of the mentor to the mentee.
- Tutoring is usually performed in a classroom, home, or public place. Mentoring is usually performed in the workplace of the mentor.

You may find that local university faculty and students are in search of community service opportunities in their field of study. These are often conditions of faculty members' employment as they work toward tenure or promotion, or in the case of college students, community service may be a course requirement. Again, although this service requirement usually connotes that it is performed free of charge, some students and faculty members may prefer to be paid for their time. Therefore, university faculty and students may be willing to tutor students without reimbursement, but this should not be your expectation.

While professors and teachers may protectively defend the little free time they have available, and some feel there is greater need for them to assist students who are struggling, rather than more advanced students, they often see the opportunity of working with advanced students as a much needed respite from the daily grind. Thus, some professional educators may see the opportunity of working with advanced K–12 students as a personally fulfilling experience; others will not.

Pinpointing costs can be difficult, as great latitude exists between what people consider their time to be worth. For college students who charge for tutorial services, you can expect to pay between $10 and $20 per hour. Rates are more variable for tutoring by university and K–12 faculty members, and you should certainly contact various teachers and professors to check their normal fees for this type of tutoring. Don't be surprised to find that most teachers and professors do not have normal rates for these somewhat unusual requests.

Unfortunately, there is rarely any correlation between the expense and the quality of the tutoring. Nor does an advanced degree automatically mean that the person knows best how to tutor your child. Most university mathematics faculty members are trained in narrow, precise fields of mathematical study. In their fields, they can provide robust enrichment opportunities for a mathematically advanced child. Unfortunately, they are often far removed from K–12 mathematics and curricula and are unable to address these needs. Conversely, many K–12 faculty members have limited mathematical backgrounds. After years of grade level teaching, many teachers are uncomfortable with mathematics that significantly surpasses what they daily encounter. Thus, the concerns of costs, while all too real for most families, should not be the most significant concern in the selection of a tutor.

After arranging for a tutor, you and your child and the selected tutor should decide what topics to cover.
- Will it be an extension of K–12 curricula or altogether different topical investigations?
- Will it deepen or broaden the curricula?
- Will it look at mathematical connections or employ projects and activities?
- Will it attempt to connect mathematical investigations with the student's already present interests?

While these types of questions will be considered in more detail in other sections, it is important to discuss them in negotiations with potential tutors.

Also, it is very important that you consider the personalities of both your child and the tutor. A mismatch of personalities can eliminate all potential gains that could have been made through the tutoring. Unfortunately, decisions regarding the personality fit between tutors and your child must be delayed until after the two meet.

Assuming that you and your child have some ideas regarding some of these

My advice to parents of gifted children is that they should be as supportive and involved as possible, and make sure the school accommodates the child whenever possible. I credit a lot of my success to the fact that when I was younger and bored, there was a special person there to work with me on advanced stuff so I did not get into trouble instead.
—University Student

previously mentioned concerns, the following subsections discuss techniques to find specific help from college students or K–12 and university faculty.

Teachers as Tutors

Connecting to teachers may be more problematic than one may imagine. Teachers' workloads are heavy and they rarely have free time to sacrifice for one student. This is even more so when the student is academically advanced. While teachers may often provide time to struggling students, successful students rarely get additional attention. This is understandable, as many teachers aim to judiciously provide assistance where they deem it most needed. Therefore, finding a teacher to support a mathematically talented child with enrichment in a home may prove difficult.

Selecting the right teacher for this relationship with your child can also be difficult. You should probably not select your child's current classroom teacher, as this may cause some difficulty in the classroom. Although it may not be possible, it may also be advantageous to your child to be partnered with a teacher unknown to his or her current classroom teacher. This would help avoid rivalries or other problems between the classroom teacher and your child's tutor.

In addition to the teacher's relationship with the student and other teachers, the teacher's mathematical background and preparation should be considered. After years of teaching grade level curriculum, not every K–12 teacher can be expected to take a student who has advanced abilities significantly beyond the mathematics they usually teach. Although their college education requires all high school mathematics teachers to have studied math significantly beyond the high school curriculum, and some take more advanced graduate mathematics courses relatively early in their teaching careers, many elementary school teachers never get to consider advanced mathematics topics in their teaching profession.

If you have decided that you would like a K–12 teacher to tutor your child, it will be helpful for you to request recommendations from the principal of your child's school or the superintendent of the school district. These administrators would know which teachers could best help your child. You should understand, however, that occasionally even administrators might not fully recognize the need for enrichment for students who are already academically advanced. Nonetheless, many administrators will be happy to assist you in this way. In addition, you should not be shy about interviewing prospective teachers. Some possible questions you should ask are:

> Math always came easily to me so I rarely asked anyone for help. In my senior year, I independently studied Calculus II with a teacher/adviser. While this independent study was valuable, I feel I missed out by not having a teacher or someone who knew the material better than I did. —High School Student

- What do you think you can offer to my child in the area of math?
- What mathematics will or should be covered?
- What instructional techniques will be used?
- How will these things differ from what would be provided in my child's school?

Professors as Tutors

Many competent mathematicians are employed at every university, college, and community college. Depending on the size of the university or college, mathematically oriented faculty members may work in various departments, such as mathematics, computer science, mathematics education, statistics, economics, or even one of the various sciences, such as physics, chemistry, and biology. Unfortunately, again, not all are a good fit for any particular child. While generally the mathematical skill of professors significantly exceeds that of K–12 mathematics teachers, many professors are out of touch with public school curricula. They are more familiar with traditional texts and course sequences, and even their teaching styles tend to be very traditional. So, most university professors may tend to be more focused on mathematical content than on student individualization.

Typically, university professors have a far more flexible schedule than K–12 teachers. Although they rarely care to maintain tutoring relationships in addition to all of their other responsibilities, they will be more willing to do so if the child is truly advanced. In fact, some who focus on cognitive issues in learning (usually mathematics education professors) may wish to provide tutorial assistance if you and your child are willing to be involved in a research study concerning the child's learning.

You should carefully examine the area of expertise of each university faculty member that you want to consider as a tutor. Although a number of mathematicians may be employed in one department, they may each have a particular topical focus. Some may have stronger backgrounds in geometry, topology, functional analysis, or statistics. Some mathematicians who have very specialized fields of study may not be interested in tutoring students through more generalized topics. Finding the appropriate tutor from the university ranks almost always begins through communication with the chairperson of the college's Department of Mathematics (or Mathematics Education—depending on the university). After a phone call or e-mail to the chairperson, he or she can then forward the entire request to faculty members who may be willing to help. If this communication does not prove fruitful, you can review the Web sites of the various departments at their local university or community college. These usually will provide adequate contact information so that you can communicate personally with each professor.

By the way, a little known secret to those outside of university academia is that departments are always looking for new and future students who will major in that field. Some resources can occasionally be diverted toward advanced students who are considering attending the university in the future.

It is important to not be intimidated by university faculty members, and you should interview potential university faculty as seriously as you would any other tutor for your child. Time commitment, expense, mathematical topics, tutoring style, and workload should all be discussed and agreed upon before any work is begun.

College Students

Seeking tutorial assistance for mathematically advanced K–12 students from college students is a gamble. It is a hit or miss proposition, because while some college students may have adequate skills to assist younger students in some topics, most will lack a vision for mathematics as a whole and lack an understanding of the numerous connections among mathematical content areas. Even though college students may know far more mathematics than that covered in K–12 curricula, they will seldom understand the complexity of national and state curriculum standards. For elementary and middle grades students, college tutors may be effective, albeit limited. However, for high school students, it is recommended that more mathematically experienced professionals be sought. If you do choose college students as tutors, you should carefully evaluate how far the college student can take your child. It is conceivable that one college student can be used to tutor one subject and another tutor be used for a different topic. If you decide that you would like to use college students as mathematics tutors, you should contact the chairperson of mathematics departments in local colleges and universities in order to request assistance in locating someone who will be an appropriate tutor.

Mentoring

If finding a competent tutor seems to be overly complex, finding a well-suited mentor may be even more difficult. Mentors for mathematically talented students tend to be professionals in fields such as mathematics, science, economics, and engineering. While per capita there are certainly many more potential mentors than there are tutors, few professionals are experienced with this type of relationship. Making the search for a mentor more complicated is that potential mentors are not housed in one institution, like a university. Rather, potential mentors can be found in virtually every company, industry, and office. However, the operative word is *potential*, as a person's mathematical expertise does not in and of itself connote an effective mathematical mentor. How, then, can you find a mentor? Mentors are usually found through social acquaintances, family members, business contacts, and so on. The people who were previously mentioned as tutors may also prove to be appropriate mentors.

Many of the same concerns for tutors apply to the selection of mentors. You should select mentors with respect to the mathematical content to be learned, schedule, and workload. Fortunately, mentoring is generally understood to be free of charge. Workplace requirements must often be considered in respect to students being mentored in professional and work settings.

You may want to look to your social and professional contacts and acquaintances to find a mentor for your mathematically advanced child. This may be a bit awkward at times, but necessary. Often the best leads are found through acquaintances.

Summary of Key Points

- There are many people in the community that you may employ to help with acceleration or enrichment in mathematics.
- Tutors may be K–12 teachers, university professors, student teachers, or college students.
- A mentor is usually a professional in a field related to mathematics such as science, economics, or engineering.
- Children should be encouraged to discover mathematics on their own.
- Connecting mathematics to other interests is one of the most powerful ways to support mathematical talent.

Question to Ask Yourself:

- How much time and money am I willing to devote to my child's pursuit of mathematics?

Questions to Ask Your Child:

- Do you wish to pursue mathematics in more depth?
- How much energy do you wish to put into this pursuit?
- Would you like to study from home or go meet with someone?

Questions to Ask Potential Tutors and Mentors:

- What are you planning to do with and show my child?
- What are your fees?
- What will you do when my child reaches either his limit or yours?

Chapter 4

Enrichment Opportunities for the Mathematically Advanced Child

n this chapter, we will consider how children can be encouraged to pursue their own investigations in mathematics. Mathematically advanced students often fare well independently of the school system. Their own interests are adequate to motivate them to continued study. Unfortunately, students occasionally need some ideas regarding how to proceed. They need to know how they can continue their studies. Among other concerns, this chapter will provide information regarding:

- mathematics-related materials;
- encouraging children to discover mathematics on their own;
- connecting mathematics to other interests;
- finding good instructional materials for children; and

- using projects, puzzles and challenges, literature, technology, competitions, field trips, and Internet resources to enrich math education.

A New Perspective
on Mathematics-Related Materials

Most people have an incorrect perspective of mathematically valuable materials. Whether for the mathematically advanced child or any other child, mathematically valuable investigations surround us daily. Hobbies, games, recreations, employment opportunities, expenditures, and countless other everyday endeavors can be mathematized. In other words, any interest, activity, or investigation can be recast as an opportunity to consider the endeavor more deeply through mathematics. In this perspective, the interest is the focal point of the mathematics. Mathematics is employed to look more deeply into and understand a person's interests. However, looking at an issue using mathematics is only one of two possible dimensions. An interest can be used to look more deeply into mathematics. Thus, mathematics becomes the focal point of the investigation, which is centered around the person's interests.

With these two dimensions in mind, it can readily be seen that worthwhile and interesting mathematics surrounds everyone every day. There is truly no need to purchase expensive books and educational materials. Although these publications may assist students in directing mathematical investigations, they are unnecessary. The only thing necessary is your child's interest in seeing things mathematically and in using those things to more deeply learn mathematics. Granted, guidance by someone who has more mathematical understanding is helpful to anyone who is studying mathematics. Nevertheless, it is the attitude and interest toward looking for opportunities to consider more mathematics that is most valuable.

Therefore, while many specific games and recreations may naturally promote mathematical understanding (e.g., Connect Four, Perfection, Monopoly, dominoes, Rubik's Cube, pattern games, chess, card games, marbles, and more) this perspective may indeed only limit you and your child from imagining a world of possible activities that can be mathematized. As mentioned many times throughout this book, a large number of Web sites can lead you to resources that will help you to consider real-world mathematics.

> I once worked for 3 full days and finally solved a specific mathematical problem. I knew an undergraduate mathematics student who was very advanced and enjoyed a challenge, so I gave him the problem to consider. After 1 hour, he returned to my office with a grin on his face. Not only had he found THREE solutions, he did so using two different techniques!
> —University Professor

Encouraging Children to Discover Mathematics on Their Own

We have considered finding external assistance either through tutors or mentors for your mathematically advanced child. But, how can you encourage your child to investigate mathematics independently, without external assistance? To begin this discussion, two points warrant mentioning. First, although costs associated with independent study may be significantly less than contracting with a tutor, this endeavor is not free. We will later discuss some anticipated costs. Second, regardless of whether tutors or mentors are used initially, it should always be the goal for mathematically advanced students to become independent learners. This learning can take many forms and be as individualized as each student.

It is important to note that those who are more psychologically, socially, and even mathematically mature usually prefer independent learning. Because traditional schooling is initially used to assist some advanced students, these resources can be expended before directing a child toward becoming an independent learner. Nevertheless, independent learning should always be the ultimate goal of all parties—parents, students, and educators. When students are learning independently it is because they have their own interest in a topic, not an interest imposed upon them by others.

Interest breeds enthusiasm, which in turn breeds skill, understanding, and further enthusiasm. We often see children who are enthralled with music, dance, art, science, sports, theater, reading, writing, and other interests. These children usually become relatively proficient in those areas in which they show interest. The same goes for math; mathematical interest breeds enthusiasm, skill, understanding, and more interest. The magic is simply finding the mathematical topics that will initially interest the student. This can be accomplished in a number of ways.

> My own interests stimulated my enthusiasm to investigate mathematical topics. I was fascinated with what my glasses were doing for my eyes and how they corrected my vision. I recall investigating radio bands in connection with my new multi-band radio. I wondered about so many aspects of the world around me and attempted to grasp them quantitatively.
> —University Mathematics Professor

Connecting Mathematics
to Common Childhood Interests

Many extracurricular interests provide wonderful opportunities for mathematical investigations for even elementary age students. Many interests lead directly to particular areas of mathematics. For example:

- Sports can lead to a study of geometry, statistics, data, measurement, probability, ratios, and percentage.
- Video games can lead to study of logic, cost-benefits analysis, algebra, data, and statistics.
- Legos™ can lead to a study of geometry and spacial relations.
- Shopping can lead to a study of percentage, ratios, algebra, systems of equations, and number systems (positive and negative).
- Receiving an allowance and counting money can lead to studies of economics, cost-benefits analysis, exponential growth, mathematical modeling, and rate of change.
- Cooking can lead to a study of measurement, ratios, proportions, geometry, spatial relations, and change.
- Bike riding can lead to the study of velocity, acceleration, changes, slope (of a hill), and ratios.
- Flying kites can lead to a study of measurement, slope, geometry, and ratios.
- Skipping rope can lead to the study of geometry, velocity, and measurement.
- Playing marbles can lead to the study of geometry, ratios, angles, and velocity.
- Art can lead to the study of geometry, change, ratios, and measurement.

Connecting Mathematics With Other Interests

Mathematics can be studied as a stand-alone subject. In and of itself, mathematics has beauty, elegance, and sophistication worthy of lifelong study. Unfortunately, in its theoretical form, most students are less interested in math. Most would like to see what mathematics could do for them. Mathematics does not reside in a vacuum isolated from other topics. Rather, mathematicians often argue that it is the glue that holds together many other interests. Students are often surprised to see how many connections there are between math and their own particular interests.

Students often have many interests outside of mathematics, and you probably know these other interests all too well. Indeed, these other interests may even be the cause of difficulties between you and your child. For instance, perhaps your child wants to spend countless hours per week playing video games. You should not quickly dismiss video games as counteractive to education, and instead you should analyze video games for their mathematical content. One mathematical field particularly important to video game players is logic. While some players may say that they are uninterested in mathematics, most will be able to correctly analyze what will happen to a certain strength rating of a character if he accomplishes, or fails to complete, a certain task. This is a combination of logic, programming, and arithmetic. The graphics on modern video games pose additional opportunities for mathematical investigations. Screen resolutions, CPU speed, memory, and bandwidth all provide opportunities for the gamer to investigate mathematical applications.

A particularly strong example of mathematics in computer games occurs in a group of games called Role Playing Games, or RPGs. In RPGs, the child interacts on the Internet with imaginary characters and other players in a setting that is dominated by math—particularly probability, statistics, and algebra. The casting of spells, creation of characters, selection of equipment, outcomes of battles, and the fate of the player are all decided based on mathematical formulas. There are no graphics, and the text can be made to scroll at a high rate of speed, allowing the child to skim the text for information. A competitive child has no choice but to learn the skills of math necessary for him to be successful in this imaginary world.

To demonstrate that mathematics can always be connected to other interests, a relatively extensive list of common interests and their ties to math is provided in Appendix H. You should show the list to your child and discuss it with her as appropriate. The mathematically advanced child will quickly recognize the richness of connections between his area of interest and mathematics.

Because it is hoped that children will become independent learners, it is important for you to be careful not to push your child into areas in which he may not be interested. You should not try to force your child to be interested in certain areas; instead, you should observe your child, find what interests him, and then guide him toward the mathematical connections associated with the interest.

> I always detested math in school, but would get up 3 hours before dawn to log into a RPG (role playing game) video game because I had found some arcane rule that made my character more powerful at certain times. Humorously, the rule was often based on the same algebra principles that I slept through in class. At 14 years old, I wanted to win the game, and if that required spending hours studying the mathematics behind its rules, I was fine with that. I'll even admit that I enjoyed the math part of the game . . . I just would not tell that to my friends.
> —University Student

Finding Good Instructional Materials for Children

Good educational materials abound and are available to parents everywhere. At nearly every bookstore, dozens of books regarding age-appropriate mathematical ideas for children are readily available. You can browse the shelves and find books that will interest your child. The Internet is also an amazing repository of stimulating mathematical ideas and materials. You certainly do not need to spend any money to access quality mathematical materials and even lesson plans regarding how best to teach certain concepts and projects that lead to deeper understanding through the Internet.

Unfortunately, this advice can be interpreted incorrectly to imply that the most valuable materials to enhance a child's learning are found in books and Web sites particularly designed to address those interests and needs. This is not necessarily the case. Newspapers, magazines, tools, gadgets, electronic devices, user manuals, encyclopedias, measuring devices, recipe books, and countless other materials that usually lie around the house can be used to generate interest in mathematics. Three pieces of simple advice can significantly assist you in finding educational materials that your child will use.

- First, you should involve your child in the selection and purchase of what sparks an interest in him or her. Do not look for what is acclaimed as *good*. Rather, watch your child and see what interests him or her. No matter how flashy, cute, or colorful the book or Web site may be, if it does not interest your child, it will have little value. Who knows how many streets could be lined with unused books that well-meaning parents have purchased for their children.

- Second, you should attempt to find ability-appropriate materials for your child. Ability appropriate does not mean either grade- or age-appropriate. Rather, it means developmentally appropriate for the mathematical level of your child. You should be cautious and avoid materials that are significantly below or above your child's ability to understand the material. Because your child is mathematically advanced, ability-appropriate materials may initially be somewhat more difficult to assess. However, after observing your child using the materials, you will soon begin to see what does and does not work and which materials are too trivial and which are too advanced.

- Third, you should use materials around the home as much as possible, particularly materials in which your child has already demonstrated interest. When *educational ideas* are continually connected to professionally produced *educational materials*, this leads children to assume that a disconnect exists between academic studies and the real world. However, when children begin to see that mathematics is innately embedded in those areas of their lives that interest them, they see how their interests and mathematics mutually work to deepen their understanding of both. Therefore, you should first look to your child's interests around the home before purchasing materials that may not hold as much interest as the child's real world.

Enrichment Through Projects

Many educators believe that students learn better by doing than by simply reading. Projects are difficult to define simply because they can take so many different forms. Children may be asked to:
- design and purchase all the materials for a new deck in the backyard,

- design an irrigation system for the garden,
- calculate the amount of fabric needed for a set of curtains, or
- determine the best organization of the furniture in their room.

You may even decide to involve your child in family financial decisions. For instance, many parents struggle annually with the calculations of their income taxes. Allow able children to help with the calculations and paperwork related to tax season. This is a valuable opportunity for children to recognize the connections between income, expenditures, taxes, deductions, mortgage interest, dependents, and the like.

Around the home, countless potential projects can bring more sophisticated mathematics into the lives of children. However, again, the projects that you select should be those that interest your child. For example, consider a family with one child who is very interested in music and another who is interested in science. To force the musician into scientific pursuits and the scientist into artistic pursuits may prove to be mostly unprofitable, because it would counter their respective natural interests. Likewise, you should find what interests your child and make progress toward the mathematical connections within that subject, and not force your child into subjects that do not interest him.

You need to be flexible and recognize what may entail a valid and valuable project for your child. While many children will not have the physical skill to aid in construction tasks or manual labor, the planning process of many projects may be greatly rewarding and enriching. Allowing mathematically advanced children to calculate the costs of repainting a room, building a porch, sewing a garment, or cooking a meal may be mathematically enriching.

Having the child monitor driving habits and mileage to schedule maintenance or assess the infinitely complex cell phone bill can also be useful endeavors.

While the home is rich with opportunity for mathematical investigation, there are also countless opportunities outside the home. Every business provides interesting mathematical investigations. You can take your child:

- to the optometrist to discuss the curvature of light;
- to the Department of Transportation to discuss traffic flow or snowplow routes;
- to an architect to discuss shape, perspective, construction, and the costing out of jobs;
- to a farm to discuss planting and weather;
- to an insurance agent to discuss insurance rates and investments;
- to a factory to discuss product flow and workforce requirements;
- to a pharmacist to discuss dosage rates and drug distribution and duration in the body; or
- to a sculptor to discuss perspective and form.

These are the types of projects that can greatly motivate children to pursue mathematical interests.

Enrichment Through Puzzles and Challenges

Many children and adults enjoy puzzles and challenges. At most bookstores, numerous books of mathematical and logical puzzles line the shelves and countless hours of recreation can be enjoyed through the use of these books. Many children enjoy this type of cognitive wrestling, and they particularly like these recreational pursuits because they are free of the stress of evaluations by teachers and grades.

You may wonder which type of puzzle book is best for your child. The answer is actually quite simple: any and all. Typical books of logic problems usually include a significant number of problems directly addressing mathematics. However, as most mathematicians know, most other logic problems can be solved by appropriately applying mathematical techniques. Occasionally, these techniques are described and explained in the back of the text. Fortunately, many of these books are provided inexpensively in paperback or on clearance racks.

One of the most popular mathematical puzzles out today is called Soduku. This is a Japanese math puzzle that provides a set of nine blocks with nine individual openings in each block. Various numbers are placed within the empty spaces to get the puzzle solver started. To complete the puzzle, solvers must place a number (from 1–9) in the remaining spaces. No single number can be repeated in each block, and numbers also cannot be repeated within rows or columns on the grid. *The New York Times* prints one of these puzzles daily on its puzzle page, and countless volumes of these puzzles can be found in bookstores and grocery stores.

> I heartily recommend the comic books, The Addventures of Plusman (correct spelling). (See http://www.plusman.org for more information.) Mathematics, science, and good old-fashioned science fiction are all wrapped up with an unending tongue-in-cheek humor. They have become very popular with advanced middle grade students who compete to find the greatest number of mathematical jokes in the story.
> —Math Teacher

More recently, books examining optical illusions are being found on the discount shelves of bookstores. Some of these examine the cognitive factors that confuse the brain and others discuss the images mathematically. These again provide interesting fodder for the mathematically advanced child.

Mathematical recreations and puzzles can greatly entertain many students. Serendipitously, while being entertained and challenged by puzzles, students often learn a great deal of mathematics. However, mathematical puzzles from Web sites, books, and magazines can be shared with all family members. Together, parents, brothers, and sisters can share puzzles and have friendly competitions. In the context of supporting a student's mathematical pursuits, the participation of entire families in mathematical puzzles can also lead to increased family cohesiveness.

Enrichment Through Literature

You may not be aware of the wide variety of nonfiction and fiction literature that now exists for various reading levels. Some mathematically focused reading exists for almost every grade level. From biographies and mathematical investigations and recreations, to mystery novels and science fiction, you can find math-related books to interest nearly every child.

A small sample of interesting mathematical reading includes:

- *A Gebra Named Al: A Novel* by Wendy Isdell
- *And He Built a Crooked House* by Robert Heinlein
- *Crushing on You* by Wendy Loggia
- *Cryptonomicon* by Neal Stephenson
- *Flatland: A Romance of Many Dimensions* by Edwin A. Abbott
- *Flatterland: Like Flatland, Only More So* by Ian Stewart
- *Permutation City* by Greg Egan
- *Spaceland: A Novel of the Fourth Dimension* by Rudy Rucker

- *Sphereland: A Fantasy About Curved Spaces and an Expanding Universe* by Dionsys Burger
- *The Number Devil: A Mathematical Adventure* by Han Magnus Enzensberger
- *The Musgrave Ritual* by Arthur Conan Doyle
- *The Planiverse: Computer Contact With a Two-Dimensional World* by A. K. Dewdney
- *The Man Who Counted* by Malba Tahan
- *Whose Side Are You On?* by Emily Moore

The following two Web sites provide excellent lists of various genres of books appropriate for various grade levels:
- http://math.cofc.edu/faculty/kasman/MATHFICT/default.html
- http://csi.boisestate.edu/dmt/mathlit.htm

In addition to books, the Internet provides countless Web sites that provide recreational reading and investigations for all age groups. Several of these Web sites are listed in the appendix of this book.

Enrichment Using Technology

As most parents already know, computers and software abound. A large number of excellent, inexpensive software programs exist for the investigation of mathematical ideas. While many software packages can be purchased at most bookstores and even department stores, many of these packages are little more than a review of mathematical subjects and courses, and we don't recommend them for home use with students who are advanced. While some of these packages provide some flexibility, most do not provoke students to investigate topics independently. Most canned packages direct students through a series of exercises not unlike what they would experience in a regular classroom. These packages may have some value for advanced mathematics students when used to allow learning of traditional courses at a more advanced pace. However, as a tool they are often unable to promote independent investigation.

Mathematics educators typically use another series of software packages designed to teach mathematical concepts and allow complete flexibility for students to independently pursue their own investigations. Most of these packages are inexpensive and can be purchased for reduced student rates. Additionally, these packages are supported through various Web sites and online discussion sites. Some excellent software packages are listed below.

> Two students were asked to explain a geometric theorem. One worked for hours on a traditional proof, only to get stuck at a critical point. One worked for a few minutes generating a diagram of the geometric idea on Geometer's Sketchpad, a software program, and the missing link in the proof was immediately recognized. —Mathematics Teacher

- *The Geometer's Sketchpad*: http://www.keypress.com/sketchpad ($39.95 for the student edition)
  Geometer's Sketchpad is a powerful tool for investigating geometric concepts. Many concepts in algebra, analytic geometry, precalculus, probability, statistics, discrete mathematics, and calculus can also be investigated through both casual and formal use. It is difficult to fully define this software, because it is simple enough to be used by primary school students and yet powerful enough to be used in high school and college mathematical investigations. Most notably, this software is very much enjoyed by students of all ages, and many students learn mathemati-

cal concepts serendipitously as they amuse themselves with the software.

- *TI-Interactive:* http://www.education.ti.com ($49.95 for student edition)
  TI Interactive, from Texas Instruments, is much more than a tool for algebraic investigations. TI Interactive can be used to discover concepts in analytic geometry, precalculus, probability, statistics, discrete mathematics, and calculus. This is a very popular software package used in high schools and universities by students and teachers. For its price, this package rivals much more expensive software. Beyond its conventional computer use, Texas Instruments has ensured that TI Interactive provides a helpful interface between the computer and many of its calculators.

- *Fathom*: http://www.keypress.com/fathom ($39.95 for student edition)
  For investigation of statistical ideas, Fathom has been proven to be exceptional. Its ease of use leads students to easily discover concepts that would typically elude them through traditional instruction and less robust statistical software.

- *Microsoft Excel*
  Fortunately, almost everyone has Microsoft Excel on his or her computer. Through countless supportive Web sites, students can use Excel to investigate mathematical concepts from numerous subject areas, including ideas in the topics of probability, statistics, algebra, calculus, discrete mathematics, and many others. Beginning in the elementary grades, Excel can be used to investigate and develop mathematical ideas. Its robust programming language also helps students prog-

ress from using simple to sophisticated Boolean logic during the investigation of mathematical behavior.

- *Programming Languages*
  Visual Basic (http://www.msdn.microsoft.com/vbasic), along with other programming languages, gives users the opportunity to investigate mathematical phenomena through logic and programming. While this is more complex than using predesigned software packages, some students find programming more fulfilling.

Another genre of software is created for the professional mathematician. These tend to simultaneously be very powerful and exceedingly expensive. Some of these include MathCad, Maple, and Mathematica, among others. These professional packages often significantly exceed the $1,000 range, so they are not recommended for family purchase and use.

Calculators are another valuable technological resource for math students. Many parents may not be familiar with the vast number of excellent advanced calculators that are available to consumers. Graphing calculators are only the beginning; more advanced calculators are also programmed with Computer Algebra Systems (CAS) that can perform symbolic algebra, precalculus, and calculus problems. CAS calculators can solve equations and simplify expressions with the press of a button. Although graphing calculators are relatively inexpensive, CAS calculators tend to be priced between $150 and $200.

Calculators today are amazingly powerful and capable of handling most topics through undergraduate mathematics. Many of the higher end calculators rival some software packages. Today's calculators are designed as tools for students to dig deeply into mathematics and independently research topics and ideas. Many of the CAS calculators also perform geometry and allow students to investigate concepts diagrammatically. In fact, few teachers and professors ever master all of the functions of these advanced calculators. Fortunately, so ubiquitous are these calculators in schools and universities today that countless Web sites provide activities and examples of their uses.

The selection between graphing calculators and CAS calculators may be difficult. Clearly, the purpose for the tool should direct the selection of the tool. Therefore, the selection of the calculator may be contingent upon the type of assistance previously decided upon. Some teachers and professors may prefer one calculator over others.

Although Casio, Hewlett Packard, Canon, and Sharp all make excellent graphing calculators, and most make CAS calculators, Texas Instruments seems to have cornered the market in mathematics education. TI calculators are excellent and popular choices. Countless independent Web sites provide applications for TI calculators. We recommend the following calculators:

- For middle grades students, the TI-73 Explorer is a terrific choice. For more information, see http://education.ti.com/us/product/tech/73/features/features.html.

- For high school students, we recommend the TI-84 Plus Silver Edition for mathematical study. However, it is not a CAS calculator. For more information on this calculator, see http://education.ti.com/us/product/tech/84pse/features/features.html.

- If you wish to purchase a CAS calculator, two are recommended: the TI-89 Titanium (see http://education.ti.com/us/product/tech/89ti/features/features.html), and the Voyage 200 (see http://education.ti.com/us/product/tech/v200/features/features.html).

Enrichment Through Field Trips

You should not underestimate the many purposes and value of field trips for your mathematically advanced child. First, field trips demonstrate the application of mathematics in many different environments and enterprises. This, in and of itself, is extremely valuable. Your child will no longer see mathematics as a static field of study, but as a living, growing, applicable endeavor. This can significantly generate interest and enthusiasm toward further study and inquisitiveness regarding the myriad of current and future applications of mathematics. Indeed, mathematics is employed all around us every day, and so much so that we often see only the forest of activity and rarely the trees of mathematical application supporting the activity. Second, observing mathematical activity can immediately generate enthusiasm among students. This enthusiasm can be twofold. Students may see applicable mathematics as a worthwhile endeavor into which he or she may wish to follow. Additionally, they may see that studying applied mathematics may lead them to discover or invent things that may better human life and productivity.

Field trips can focus on the innate interests of your child or purposefully bring the child into an unfamiliar arena in order to extend the child's experiences. Of course, science and mathematics museums make for excellent field trips. But, these opportunities are often restricted to more urban environments where these museums exist. Hundreds of other opportunities surround all families.

> My father took me to the local paper mill for a tour of the entire paper-making process, from debarking lumber, to huge rolls of paper coming off paper machines. We watched as paper thickness, density, finish, wetness, and many other factors were continually monitored and maintained. I was filled with awe over the entire experience.
> —Math Teacher

Farms, factories, museums, workplaces, and countless other environments can be valuable field trips.

Enrichment Through Speakers

There is also value in bringing your mathematically talented child to hear mathematical speakers. Countless speakers present talks at universities, and local, state, regional, national, and international conferences each year. Student registration fees for most conferences are negligible, and often waived completely. Most universities have regular guest lectures. Unfortunately, the general public is usually unaware of local conferences and invited speakers. Information regarding these activities usually can be found through the mathematics department of a local university.

In addition to attending the presentations of others, you may wish to join other parents to collaborate and invite university faculty to come to a multifamily meeting to present a talk. Many faculty members would be pleased to do this as an outreach and potential recruitment tool.

Enrichment Through Textbooks

The history of mathematics is replete with the stories of famous mathematicians who became interested in mathematics by sneaking glimpses into their parents' or older siblings' mathematical textbooks. Being surrounded by mathematical resources seems to be the key to whetting the appetite for many aspiring mathematicians. Although resources are readily and continually available today on the Internet, many people still feel more personally connected to an actual textbook. Thus, it is recommended that you supply your child with an adequate supply of mathematical textbooks on varying levels and subjects.

The nonmathematician may not realize how many fields of mathematics exist. Nor will one know the great diversity in knowledge and fields that different mathematicians possess. While one mathematician may be a geometer, another may be an algebraist. Even within these fields, there is great latitude. This also connotes that mathematics textbooks are published in countless subjects and specializations. Thus, not every textbook is appropriate for young, albeit advanced, students. You may wish to seek guidance from teachers and professors regarding the appropriateness of certain texts.

Often, different textbooks on the same topic differ regarding their focus and direction. Different algebra texts may focus on technology, applications, or the notion of function. Different authors also present different writing styles. Some students may like certain styles more than others.

Reading textbooks brings a number of educational benefits to students. First, students grow by reading literature from a certain genre. Students learn the writing style of mathematics. They learn how mathematicians communicate complex ideas through concise and precise language. Second, reading mathematics helps students learn how to communicate mathematical ideas to others. Thus, reading mathematical texts helps to develop students as both consumers and communicators of mathematics.

At this point, you may be put off, assuming that the exorbitant costs of textbooks (usually $80–$120) will make getting them for your child beyond your financial reach. This is not the case. Extras of past edition textbooks are available in every university mathematics department. Faculty members regularly have many on their shelves they usually discard with time, and are quite willing to donate them to families in this kind of need. Used book sales are usually well-stocked with mathematics texts. Libraries also hold any number of mathematics books for loan. With a little investigation, you will be surprised at the number of mathematics texts you can obtain with little or no money.

When searching for mathematics textbooks, it is important for you to know that it is not necessary to get the newest textbooks published. Old textbooks work well also. While the newer textbooks tend to integrate more technology into the discussions, the older texts often demonstrate techniques infrequently seen today.

Enrichment Using the Internet

Mathematical Puzzles on the Internet

The Internet is full of Web sites focusing on mathematical puzzles for students of all ages. A simple Google search of the phrase *math puzzles* produces hundreds of hits, probably far more than many families would wish to investigate. Below are a few examples of excellent Web sites that offer numerous math puzzles for both learning and entertainment.

- http://www.cut-the-knot.org
- http://www.mathpuzzle.com
- http://mathforum.org/k12/k12puzzles
- http://www.k111.k12.il.us/king/math.htm
- http://www.aimsedu.org/puzzle
- http://www.math.utah.edu/~cherk/puzzles.html
- http://www.coolmath4kids.com
- http://www.qbyte.org/puzzles

- http://campuscgi.princeton.edu/~mathclub/index.pl
- http://www.mathpower.com/funstuff.htm
- http://thinks.com/webguide/mathpuzzles.htm
- http://www.galileo.org/math/puzzles.html

Webquests and Applets

Many resources are available on the Internet for students to further investigate mathematical concepts. Webquests are becoming very popular, as students can follow directions through a series of Web sites to investigate a mathematical concept. A Google™ search of the phrase *Webquests* will provide numerous valuable results. Generally, students find Web quests to be both interesting and enjoyable.

The Internet also provides a number of sites with applets that are designed to investigate mathematical concepts. There are already hundreds of these Web sites with more becoming available daily. The following list will give you a place to begin:

- http://webquest.sdsu.edu
- http://www.edinformatics.com/il/il_math.htm
- http://www.walter-fendt.de/m14e
- http://smard.cqu.edu.au/Database/Teaching/JavaMath.html
- http://archives.math.utk.edu/cgi-bin/interactive.html
- http://www.analyzemath.com
- http://users.pandora.be/educypedia/education/mathematicsjavageometry.htm
- http://www.ies.co.jp/math/java

The National Council of Teachers of Mathematics Illuminations site provides numerous math investigations that can be accessed by anyone with a computer connected to the

Internet (http://www.illuminations.nctm.org). The National Library of Virtual Manipulatives for Interactive Mathematics (http://www.matti.usu.edu/nlvm/nav/vlibrary.html) provides a rich assortment of applets for mathematical investigations. Both the Illuminations site and the Library site provide applets for mathematical investigations organized by both grade and mathematical subject.

A number of Web sites have begun to catalog the numerous software products created for the study of mathematics. One of the most extensive lists of titles may be found at the University of Haifa Web site (http://math.haifa.ac.il/msoftware.html).

Enrichment Through Summer Camps

As with other interests, an ever-increasing number of summer camps are designed to meet the needs and interests of mathematically advanced children. Because summer camps are usually localized and regional, it is impossible to provide an adequate list in this section. Parents are recommended to contact their local university mathematics department to inquire what may be available in their area.

Summer camps are usually exploratory in nature. Participants work collaboratively on various mathematics and science problems over the course of a number of days. Mathematically advanced students generally find these activities very rewarding.

Parents, you should be very certain that your child will appreciate being away at a camp for a week or more before enrolling her in such activities. Not all children desire such opportunities. Indeed, many mathematically advanced students want to do little to further advertise their difference from their friends. Thus, care for your child's psyche must be balanced with the potential of a stimulating and rewarding endeavor.

Enrichment Through Mathematical Competitions

While some children loathe competition and prefer to avoid such stress, others thrive on the excitement of competition and seek its stimulation. Mathematical competitions are becoming more popular, and local, state, and national competitions provide mathematically advanced students with opportunities to meet others with similar interests and talents. Again, parents, you must be careful not to push your child into competitions if he does not desire to do such things. Competitions are not for everyone.

> My interest in math was really sparked by competitions. Up until high school, I was competent in math, but not particularly interested. But, starting in 9th grade, I participated in a bunch of competitions and really enjoyed them. In these competitions, one usually has all the mathematical knowledge necessary to solve most problems, but applying that knowledge is much more challenging.
> —University Student

There is no ironclad technique for preparing for mathematical competitions. Each competition focuses on different mathematical aspects. While a student may be able to prepare for a given competition, he could not prepare for them all. As a student becomes more involved in any competition, he will become aware of the mathematical focus of the competitions and be able to direct his studies in the proper mathematical topics.

A list of mathematical competitions is provided in Appendix A. Parents and students should be able to find a competition that interests them.

Summary of Key Points

- Puzzles, challenges, and competitions are fun for all ages, and often spark a child's interest in a different area of mathematics.
- Many nonfiction and fiction books have been written that focus on mathematics, and these may be particularly enjoyable for mathematically advanced students.
- A great deal of high-quality software is available for home use for computers and calculators.
- You should utilize field trips, lectures on mathematical topics, and a variety of textbooks to enrich your child's mathematical experience.

Questions to Ask Your Child

- Do you like to do math by yourself or with others?
- Do you enjoy computer games, puzzle books, or story books about math?
- What kinds of projects do you enjoy? Do you like to construct or build things?
- Are there particular careers that seem to be interesting that you would like to know more about?
- Would you enjoy hearing a mathematician speak about an area of math?
- Do you enjoy mathematics competitions?

Questions to Ask Yourself

- Would you like to include your child in some of the everyday applications of mathematics that you use frequently?
- Are there projects that your child could do with you that include mathematics?
- Would you enjoy taking your child on field trips to encourage his mathematics development?
- Can you provide your child with sufficient access to the Internet so she can take advantage of some the mathematics information that is available there?

Conclusion

We hope that this book has been helpful to you. The remainder of the book is simply a list of resources for parents and students. Some of these resources generically consider gifted education and others more precisely address mathematics and mathematics education. Hopefully, these too will be found helpful.

Appendix A

Contests and Competitions

American Mathematics Competition (AMC)

P.O. Box 839400, University of Nebraska-Lincoln, Lincoln, NE 68583-9400

http://www.unl.edu/amc

Any student who has not graduated from high school is eligible for this contest. Students who perform well may move on to the American Invitational Mathematics Exam, USA Mathematical Olympiad, and International Mathematical Olympiad.

American Regions Mathematics League (ARML)

4505-6 Staffordshire Dr., Wilmington, NC 28412

http://arml.com

High school students may compete in this annual mathematics competition that is held at three sites: Penn State University, University of Iowa, and San Jose State University.

Future Problem Solving Program

2028 Regency Road, Lexington, KY 40503-2309

http://www.fpsp.org
Provides both competitive and noncompetitive problem-solving activities and activities in creative problem solving.

Intel Science Talent Search (formerly the Westinghouse Science Talent Search)
1719 N St. NW, Washington, DC 20036
http://www.sciserv.org/sts
College scholarships are awarded based on independent research projects.

Junior Engineering Technical Society (JETS)
1420 King St., Ste. 405, Alexandria, VA 22314
http://www.jets.org
Designed to promote interest in engineering, science, mathematics, and technology, JETS is a national educational organization that provides competitions and programs to high school students.

MATHCOUNTS
1420 King St., Alexandria, VA 22314
http://www.mathcounts.org
A competitive, four-stage, yearlong program catered to seventh and eighth graders. The National Society of Professional Engineers, the National Council of Teachers of Mathematics, NASA, and the CNA Foundation administer this program jointly.

Mathematical Olympiads for Elementary and Middle School (MOEMS)
2154 Bellmore Ave., Bellmore, NY 11710-5645
http://www.moems.org

Students in grades 4–8 may participate in this in-school academic year competition. The program is broken into two divisions: E for grades 4–6, and M for grades 6–8.

National Merit Scholarships

1560 Sherman Ave., Ste. 200, Evanston, IL 60201-4897

http://www.nationalmerit.org

Winners receive college scholarships based on PSAT scores.

Science Olympiad

5955 Little Pine Lane, Rochester, MI 48306

http://www.soinc.org

Provides competitions, classroom activities, and training workshops for students and teachers. This program is designed to enhance interest in and the quality of science education.

U.S. Chemistry Team (High School)

American Chemical Society, Education Division,

1155 16th St. NW, Washington, DC 20036

http://www.chemistry.org

Multitiered competition designed to promote interest and achievement in high school chemistry. ACS provides local competitions and a national, three-part exam.

U.S. Physics Team (High School)

American Association of Physics Teachers, American Center for Physics

Programs and Conferences Department, One Physics Ellipse, College Park, MD 20740-3845

http://www.aapt.org/Contests/olympiad.cfm

High school students compete to represent the U.S. at the International Physics Olympiad competition.

Appendix B
Early Entrance to College Programs

Accelerated College Entrance Center
California State University, Sacramento (grades 9–12)
6000 J St., Sacramento, CA 95819-6098
http://www.educ.csus.edu/projects/ace
Enables highly qualified students to attend California State University, Sacramento and earn college credits while completing their high school education.

The Advanced Academy of Georgia
Honors House, State University of West Georgia
1600 Maple St., Carrollton, GA, 30118-5130
http://www.advancedacademy.org
Residential early entrance to college program for gifted or highly talented students who would have been juniors or seniors had they remained in high school.

The Clarkson School
P.O. Box 5650, Potsdam, NY 13699-5650

http://www.clarkson.edu/tcs
Early entrance program for highly qualified students who have completed 11th grade to enroll at Clarkson University.

The National Academy of Arts, Sciences, and Engineering at the University of Iowa
http://www.education.uiowa.edu/belinblank/programs/naase
For high school students who have completed the equivalent of 11th grade.

Program for the Exceptionally Gifted
Mary Baldwin College, Staunton, VA 24401
http://www.mbc.edu/peg
Girls may apply to this program as early as the eighth grade; students generally complete their bachelor's degree within 4 years.

Simon's Rock
Director of Admission, Simon's Rock of Bard College
84 Alford Road, Great Barrington, MA 01230
http://www.simons-rock.edu
Students who have completed 10th grade may qualify for admittance. This program is the nation's only college of the liberal arts and sciences expressly designed for high school age students.

Halbert and Nancy Robinson Center for Young Scholars
University of Washington, Guthrie Annex
P.O. Box 351630, Seattle, WA 98195
http://www.depts.washington.edu/cscy
Provides various opportunities for gifted students.

Appendix C
Internet Mathematics Resources for Students

Ask Dr. Math
http://www.mathforum.org/dr.math
Provides assistance for elementary, middle, high school, and college students. Math topics include, but are not limited to, algebra and geometry.

Cool Math
http://www.coolmath.com
This site provides math games, lessons, and puzzles for students. This site also contains resources for parents and teachers.

Funbrain
http://www.funbrain.com
Math games for students.

Interactive Math Activities
http://www.cut-the-knot.org/Curriculum
Puzzles and games enable students to improve their skills in memory, math, algebra, and logic.

Math Forum Student Center

http://www.mathforum.org/students
Math resource site for elementary, middle, high school, undergraduate, and graduate students. There are also sites for parents
and teachers.

Math Games

http://www.madras.fife.sch.uk/maths/activities.html
Math games and resources for students, parents, and teachers.
This site also has an archives section.

Mega-Math

http://wwwc3.lanl.gov/mega-math
This site is designed to enable teachers to introduce innovative
mathematical ideas to elementary school children.

Set

http://www.setgame.com
This site contains a daily puzzle section. Parents may also purchase products from this site.

Appendix D
Internet Resources for Parents

"If Dr. Seuss Had a Gifted Child"
http://www.hoagiesgifted.org/gifted_seuss.htm

Gifted 101: A Guide for First Time Visitors
http://www.hoagiesgifted.org/gifted_101.htm

Gifted 102: The Next Steps
http://www.hoagiesgifted.org/gifted_102.htm

You Know You're the Parent of a Gifted Child When . . .
http://www.hoagiesgifted.org/parent_of.htm

The Ridiculous Things I Heard Today
http://www.hoagiesgifted.org/ridiculous_things.htm

Parent Resource to a Variety of Topics
http://www.hoagiesgifted.org/parents.htm

Success Stories in Gifted Education
http://www.hoagiesgifted.org/success_stories.htm

"Is It a Cheetah?" by Stephanie S. Tolan—Analogy to Highly Gifted Children
http://www.stephanietolan.com/is_it_a_cheetah.htm

Existential Depression in Gifted Students
http://www.giftedbooks.com/aart_webb2.html

Appendix E
Gifted Education Organizations

Most states have a state organization to promote advocacy for gifted and talented students at the state and local level, provide preservice and in-service training in gifted education, and support parent/community awareness, education, and involvement. See the National Association for Gifted Children Web site (http://www.nagc.org) for specific information.

American Association for Gifted Children
Duke University, P.O. Box 90270, Durham, NC 27708-0270
http://www.aagc.org
The AAGC was established in the late 1940s, and is the nation's oldest advocacy organization for gifted children.

The Association for the Gifted (TAG)
1110 North Glebe Road, Ste. 300, Arlington, VA 22201
http://www.cectag.org
A branch of the Council for Exceptional Children (CEC).

Hollingworth Center for Highly Gifted Children
827 Center Ave. #282, Dover, NH 03820-2506
http://www.hollingworth.org
A national, volunteer service that provides resources and support to gifted students, their families, schools, and communities.

National Association for Gifted Children
1707 L St. NW, Ste. 550, Washington, DC 20036
http://www.nagc.org
NAGC is a nonprofit organization that hosts an annual convention and publishes two periodicals—a magazine for parents (*Parenting for High Potential*) and a journal for professionals (*Gifted Child Quarterly*).

National Foundation for Gifted and Creative Children
395 Diamond Hill Road, Warwick, RI 02886
http://www.nfgcc.org
NFGCC is a nonprofit organization that emphasizes the prevailing dangers of overprescribing drugs to gifted and creative children.

Pre-K–12 Gifted Program Standards
http://www.nagc.org/index.aspx?id=546
This site contains seven tables covering curriculum and instruction, program design, program evaluation, program administration and management, socioemotional guidance and counseling, professional development and student identification.

Supporting Emotional Needs of the Gifted (SENG)
P.O. Box 6550, Scottsdale, AZ 85261
http://www.sengifted.org
Provides resources and support with the intent of providing optimal learning environments for gifted children.

Appendix F
Periodicals for Parents

Gifted Child Quarterly
National Association for Gifted Children (NAGC)
http://www.nagc.org
The quarterly journal of the NAGC contains articles of interest to professionals and those with a basic understanding of the field of gifted education.

Gifted Child Today
Prufrock Press, Inc.
http://www.prufrock.com
Suited to parents and educators, this magazine provides practical advice on working with gifted, creative, and talented children.

Imagine
Center for Talented Youth at Johns Hopkins University
http://www.jhu.edu/~gifted/imagine
A magazine for academically talented students.

Journal for the Education of the Gifted
The Association for the Gifted (TAG), a division of the Council for Exceptional Children
http://www.prufrock.com
Journal designed for authorities in the field of gifted education.

Parenting for High Potential
National Association for Gifted Children (NAGC)
http://www.nagc.org
A comprehensive magazine designed for parents of gifted, creative, and talented children.

Roeper Review
The Roeper School
http://www.roeper.org
Provides research-based articles that examine both theoretical and practical issues concerning gifted individuals.

Understanding Our Gifted
Open Space Communications, Inc.
http://www.our-gifted.com
Quarterly journal published for parents, teachers, and counselors of gifted, creative, and talented students.

Vision
The Connie Belin & Jacqueline N. Blank International Center for Gifted Education and Talent Development, The University of Iowa
http://www.education.uiowa.edu/belinblank
Published twice a year, this newsletter describes the programs and services offered by the Belin-Blank International Center for Gifted Education and Talent Development.

Appendix G
Talent Searches

Academic Talent Search

School of Education, California State University, 6000 J St., Sacramento, CA 95819-6098

http://edweb.csus.edu/projects/ATS

Conducts talent searches, as well as summer and weekend programs for students in grades 6–9. Based in the Sacramento area, this program provides challenging courses to gifted and motivated students.

ADVANCE Program for Young Scholars

P.O. Box 5671, Natchitoches, LA 71497

http://www.advanceprogram.org

Provides an intensive summer program for gifted, creative, and talented students ranging from 12 to 17 years old in grades 7–11.

Belin-Blank International Center for Gifted Education and Talent Development

600 Blank Honors Center, The University of Iowa, Iowa City, IA 52242-0454

http://www.education.uiowa.edu/belinblank
Talent search (Belin-Blank Exceptional Student Talent Search, or BESTS) for grades 2–9 and commuter and residential programs for grades 3–12. Provides above-level testing in order to determine the appropriate level of academic challenge needed for student growth.

Canada/USA Mathcamp
129 Hancock St., Cambridge, MA 02139
http://www.mathcamp.org
An intensive 5-week-long summer program for mathematically talented high school students, ages 13–18.

Carnegie Mellon Institute for Talented Elementary Students (C-MITES)
4902 Forbes Ave., Carnegie Mellon University, Pittsburgh, PA 15213
http://www.cmu.edu/cmites
Provides elementary student talent search testing at 50 sites and summer programs at 33 sites throughout Pennsylvania.

Center for Talent Development
School of Education and Social Policy, Northwestern University, 617 Dartmouth Place, Evanston, IL 60208
http://www.ctd.northwestern.edu
Talent searches for grades 4–9, and summer and weekend programs, both commuter and residential, for grades K–12. The Center for Talent Development also provides support and resources to thousands of gifted students throughout the Midwest.

Center for Talented Youth (CTY)

Johns Hopkins University, 5801 Smith Ave. #400 McAuley Hall, Baltimore, MD 21209

http://www.cty.jhu.edu

Provides commuter and residential programs for elementary and secondary students.

Frances A. Karnes Center for Gifted Studies

The University of Southern Mississippi, Box 8207, Hattiesburg, MS 39406-8207

http://www.usm.edu/~gifted

Provides support and resources for gifted students in grades K–12.

Hampshire College Summer Studies in Mathematics

Hampshire College, Amherst, MA

http://www.hcssim.org

Intensive summer mathematics program for gifted high school students.

Math for Young Achievers (MYA)

University of Wisconsin at Eau Claire, Eau Claire, WI

http://www.uwec.edu/ce/youth/math/description.htm

Office of Precollegiate Programs for Talented and Gifted (OPP-TAG)

357 Carver Hall, Iowa State University, Ames, IA 50011-2060

http://www.public.iastate.edu/~opptag_info

Provides residential summer classes in a variety of subjects for gifted, creative, and talented students in grades 7–9.

Pennsylvania Governor's Schools of Excellence
333 Market St., Harrisburg, PA 17126
http://www.pde.state.pa.us/excellence
Summer residential programs for artistically or academically talented high school students who have completed grades 10 or 11.

Program in Mathematics for Young Scientists (PROMYS)
Dept. of Mathematics, Boston University
111 Cummington St., Boston, MA 02215
http://math.bu.edu/people/promys
Supportive 6-week-long summer program held at Boston University. The purpose of this program is to stimulate mathematically talented high school students.

Purdue University Gifted Education Resource Institute (GERI)
Beering Hall, 100 N. University St., Purdue University, West Lafayette, IN 47907-2067
http://www.geri.soe.purdue.edu
Located at Purdue University, this program researches the psychological aspects of gifted education.

Research Science Institute, Center for Excellence in Education
8201 Greensboro Dr., Ste. 215, McLean, VA 22102
http://www.cee.org/rsi
An intensive 6-week-long program emphasizing advanced theory and research in mathematics, science, and engineering.

Rocky Mountain Talent Search and Summer Institute (RMTS)
1981 S. University Blvd., Denver, CO 80208
http://www.du.edu/education/ces/rmts.html
Located at the University of Denver, RMTS provides stimulat-

ing programs for academically gifted fifth- through ninth-grade students in a seven state region.

Ross Mathematics Program
Dept. of Mathematics, Ohio State University, 231 W. 18th Ave., Columbus, OH 43210
http://www.math.ohio-state.edu/ross
Intense program for 14- to 17-year-olds gifted in mathematics and science.

Southern Methodist University Gifted Students Institute and Precollege Programs
The Gifted Students Institute, Southern Methodist University
P.O. Box 750383, Dallas, TX 75275-0383
http://www.smu.edu/continuing_education/youth/gsi
Provides summer and year-round programs for gifted precollege students grades 7–11.

Summer Program for Verbally and Mathematically Precocious Youth
The Center for Gifted Studies at Western Kentucky University, 1906 College Heights Blvd. #71031, Bowling Green, KY 42101
http://www.wku.edu/gifted
Provides support and services for academically gifted and talented students in grades 7–10. The Center for Gifted Students also provides support and services to teachers and parents.

Talent Identification Program (TIP)
Duke University, 1121 West Main St., Durham, NC 27701-2028
http://www.tip.duke.edu
Residential summer program for grades 7–12, and educational

information provided to students in grades 4–6. TIP provides challenging 3-week-long courses for academically gifted students in grades 7–10.

Wisconsin Center for Academically Talented Youth (WCATY)

2909 Landmark Place, Madison, WI 53713

http://www.wcaty.org

WCATY provides challenging online courses through the school year and residential programs in the summer.

University of Minnesota Talented Youth Mathematics Program (UMTYMP)

Institute of Technology Center for Educational Programs, 4 Vincent Hall

206 Church St. SE, University of Minnesota, Minneapolis, MN 55455

http://www.math.umn.edu/itcep/umtymp

Commuter program in accelerated mathematics for grades 5–12. UMTYMP provides challenging educational opportunities to gifted students enrolled in grades 5–12 throughout Minnesota.

Appendix H
Real-World Interests Involving Mathematics

To demonstrate that mathematics can always be connected to other interests, the following list is provided. Parents should show the list to their children and discuss it with them, as appropriate. The mathematically advanced child will quickly recognize the richness of connections between his or her area of interest and mathematics.

Agriculture and math
- planting cycles
- plotting fields

Algebra
- algebraic fallacies
- algebraic models
- algebraic recreations
- conic sections
- complex numbers
- cubics and quartics
- curves of constant width
- cycloids
- graphing complex roots
- negative numbers
- partial fractions
- proofs of algebraic theorems
- Pythagorean triples
- theory of equations

Architecture and math
- drafting
- CAD
- orthinographics
- Golden Rectangle
- parabolic rooms
- St. Louis Arch

Arithmetic
- arithmetic fallacies
- arithmetic recreations
- calculating shortcuts

checking arithmetic
operations
Art and math
chromatology
Four Color Problem
fractals
history
painting
perspective
sculpting
Automotive
engine displacement
gas mileage
horsepower
performance
RPMs
tire wear
torque
wheel alignment
Banking
annuities
banker's rule
check balancing
prime interest rate
simple and compound
interest
Boolean algebra
binary arithmetic
set theory
switching theory
Brocard points
Business

adjustment for inflation
break even analysis
expected profit
gross national product
market index
percent markup and
markdown
prime interest rate
project management
stock market
Calculators
Calculus
areas and volumes
differentiation
gravitation
higher order curves
integration
optimization
Careers in mathematics
Cavalieri's Theorem
Comic strip math
Communication and math
analog and digital
Morse Code
postal service
radio
step functions
telephone
television
Computers
abacus
analog computer

ASCII
  binary computer
  fuzzy logic
  slide rule
Consumer affairs
  appreciation of a house
  automobile insurance
  exchange rates
  inflation
  items on sale
  lotteries
  mailing
  product warranties
  renting vs. buying
Continued fractions
Cylindrical projections
Decision making
  fuzzy logic
  linear programming
  logic
  reasoning
Cryptography
  encryption
  prime numbers
Desargues' Theorem
Duality
Dynamic symmetry
Ecology
  acid rain
  clean-up costs
  endangered species
  hypoxia

nuclear waste
ozone
pesticides
pollution
population flux
rates of destruction
reclamation costs
recycling
toxicity
Education and math
  educators
  epistemology
  history
  manipulatives
  pedagogy
  problem making
  problem solving
  teacher education
Euler Line
Exponentiation
  decay
  growth
  king and chess board
  logarithms
  Richter Scale
Extension of Euler's Formula
  to N Dimensions
Extension of Pappus's
  Theorem
Fibonacci numbers
Finite differences
Finite mathematics

combinatorics
networks
Pascal's Theorem
probability
Stochastic Processes
Forces and math
centrifugal
centripetal
gravitation
heat
kinesthetic
kinetic
motion
tangential
tensor
vectors
Four Color Problem
Fractals
art
chaos
Gaming and math
economics
expectation
game theory
odds
probability
Gaussian Primes
Geodesics
Geography
cartography
climate
great circles

Greenwich Mean Time
International Date Line
longitude and latitude
Geometry
cylindrical projections
Euclidean
nonEuclidean
Advanced Euclidean
    Geometry
differential geometry
finite geometry
fractals
five point circle
geometry constructions
geodesics
geometric
dissections—tangrams
fourth dimension
geometric fallacies
geometric models
geometric stereograms
geometric transformations
geometry of bubbles and
    liquid film
geometry of catenary
intuitive geometric
    recreations
Lobachevskian Geometry
maximum-minimum in
    geometry
projective geometry
regular polygons

Industry and math
  construction
  robotics
  transportation
Integration
Inventions and math
Legislation and math
Literature and math
Linear algebra
  determinants
  matrices
Linear programming
Lissajou's figures
Magic square construction
Map projections
Mascheroni's Constructions
Mathematicians
  Asian
  Black
  European
  Indian
  men
  modern
  Muslim
  women
Measurement
Medicine
  epidemiology
  genetics
  immunology
  pharmacology
Meteorology

Metric system
Military uses
Minimal surfaces
Modulo arithmetic in
  algebra
Money and math
  accounting
  banking
  business
  consumerism
  economics
  interest
  investment
  life insurance
  insurance
  marketing
  real estate
  stock market
  taxes
Multinomial theorem
Music and math
  instruments
  oscillations
  pythagoreans
  sound waves
  theory
Napier's rods
Nature and mathematics
Networks
  linear programming
  discrete optimization
Nine point circle

Number theory
> bases other than ten
> continued fractions
> Diophantine equations
> divisibility of numbers
> elementary number theory
>> applications
> extension of Euler's
>> Theorem
> Fermat's Last Theorem
> Gaussian primes
> number theory proofs
> polygonal numbers
> perfect numbers
> prime numbers

Numerology

Optometry

Patterns
> Fibonacci numbers
> finite differences

Philosophy and math
> cosmology
> eschatology
> math education

Probability
> Monte Carlo method
> multiple choice tests

Pure math

Recreation and math
> brain games
> magic squares
> puzzles

Regular polyhedra

Religion and math

Research

Science and math
> aeronautics
> archeology
> astronomy
> atmospheric pressure
> aviation
> bioclamatic rule
> biology
> botany
> carbon dating
> chemistry
> crystallography
> ecology
> electricity and magnetism
> electricity and resistance
> electronics
> energy
> engineering
> fluid dynamics
> forestry
> genetics
> gravity
> half-life and decay
> light
> mass
> noise and anti-noise
> nuclear power
> nutrition
> oceanography

optics
optometry
pressure
radiation
relativity
seismology
space
weather
weight

Sequences and series
arithmetic
Fibonacci numbers
geometric
harmonic
Nth term
sum of N terms

Set theory

Social opinions and math

Social studies and math
criminology

Solid geometry

Sports and math

Statistics
actuarial studies
census information
death/dying
elections
estimation
familial
intelligence quotients
least squares
marriage/divorce

means
nonparametric statistics
penology
population
poverty

Structural dynamics
flexagons
geodesics

Surveying

Time
ancient
calendars
carbon dating
oscillations

Topology
paper folding

Trigonometry
Spherical trigonometry

Transcendental numbers

Weight

References

Assouline, S. G., Colangelo, N., Lupkowski-Shoplik, A. E., Lipscomb, J., & Forstadt, L. (2003). *Iowa acceleration scale 2nd edition: A guide to whole-grade acceleration K–8.* Scottsdale, AZ: Great Potential Press.

Assouline, S., & Lupkowski-Shoplik, A. (2005). *Developing math talent: A guide for challenging and educating gifted students.* Waco, TX: Prufrock Press.

Karnes, F. A., & Marquardt, R. G. (1991a). *Gifted children and the law: Mediation, due process and court cases.* Dayton, OH: Ohio Psychology Press.

Karnes, F. A., & Marquardt, R. G. (1991b). *Gifted children and legal issues in education: Parents' stories of hope.* Dayton, OH: Ohio Psychology Press.

Karnes, F. A. & Marquardt, R. G. (2000). *Gifted children and legal issues: An update.* Scottsdale, AZ: Gifted Psychology Press.

National Association for Gifted Students (NAGC). (1998). *Gifted program standards.* Retrieved October 26, 2005, from http://www.nagc.org/index.aspx?id_546

National Council of Teachers of Mathematics (NCTM). (2000). *Principles and standards for school mathematics*. Reston, VA: Author.

National Council of Teachers of Mathematics (NCTM). (2005). *Closing the achievement gap*. Retrieved November 14, 2005, from http://www.nctm.org/about/position_statements/position_achievementgap.htm

No Child Left Behind Act, 20 U.S.C. §6301 (2001).

U. S. Department of Education, Office of Educational Research and Improvement. (1993). *National excellence: A case for developing America's talent*. Washington, DC: U.S. Government Printing Office.

About the Authors

Michael J. Bossé has been involved in teacher preparation, professional development, and the education of K–12 students for more than 15 years. As a university faculty member, Mike has been teaching future mathematics teachers and working on various projects with public school administrators, teachers, parents, and students throughout his career. He currently serves as associate professor of math and science education at East Carolina University in Greenville, NC. Mike earned both his bachelor's and masters' degrees from Southern Connecticut State University and his Ph.D. from the University of Connecticut.

Mike's interests in children span the grades and all ability levels. As a university professor, he continues to serve the educational community by working with teachers and students and creating learning opportunities and curricula that involve, interest, and challenge a full range of students. His numerous publications also address issues throughout the realm of mathematics education. He continues to seek outlets for his voracious appetite for writing and for serving mathematics education both locally and nationally.

Mike plans to continue to write and produce materials for all levels of mathematics education. He is currently working on a number of projects—writing and developing books, curricula, and electronic media. Continuously supported by his wife, Rocky, and his children, Mike continues to actively seek how he may better meet the needs of K–12 mathematics teachers and students through the coming decades.

Jennifer V. Rotigel has been involved in education for 30 years as a parent, teacher, consultant, and university professor. Jennie's career has included teaching children of a wide variety of ages and abilities in the areas of early childhood, elementary education, special education, and gifted education. She has spent her academic career at Indiana University of Pennsylvania (IUP) in the area of teacher preparation where she is associate professor and chair of the Department of Professional Studies in Education. Jennie earned both her M.Ed. and Ed.D. degrees from Indiana University of Pennsylvania.

Jennie has dedicated her professional career to the notion that all children should enjoy learning and be able to learn something new and exciting every day. This has led her to spend much time in the development of new programs and curricula, designing instructional plans and teacher training workshops, and writing journal articles and book chapters. Her advocacy activities have convinced many of the need to establish a system of education in which every child (including those with advanced ability) is able to learn at his or her individual level and pace.

As the mother of four boys, Jennie has developed a special interest in helping parents to understand and meet their children's educational needs. She hopes that parents who read this book will benefit from her experiences in raising mathematically talented children. Her work is supported by her husband, Dave, her close-knit family, and her colleagues at IUP.